Collins

11+

Verbal Reasoning Cloze

Support & Practice Workbook

Chris Pearse, Louise Swann
and Hilary Male

Published by Collins
An imprint of HarperCollins*Publishers* Ltd
1 London Bridge Street
London SE1 9GF

HarperCollins*Publishers*
1st Floor, Watermarque Building, Ringsend Road, Dublin 4, Ireland

ISBN 978-0-00-849740-8

First published 2021

10 9 8 7 6 5 4 3 2 1

British Library Cataloguing in Publication Data.
A CIP record of this book is available from the British Library.
Commissioning: Clare Souza
Authors: Chris Pearse, Louise Swann and Hilary Male
Project Management: Richard Toms and Sundus Pasha
Cover Design: Kevin Robbins and Sarah Duxbury
Inside Concept Design: Ian Wrigley
Typesetting and artwork: Jouve India Private Limited
Production: Karen Nulty

The Butterfly Lion (by Michael Morpurgo) extract is reprinted
by permission of HarperCollins*Publishers* Ltd © Morpurgo (1996)

The *War Horse* (by Michael Morpurgo) extract is reprinted
by permission of HarperCollins*Publishers* Ltd © Morpurgo (2007)

Some texts have been adapted for the purpose of the exercises in the book.

Published in collaboration with Teachitright.
Billy the Bookworm™ is the property of Teachitright Ltd.

Printed in the United Kingdom.

Contents

Introduction   **5**

SECTION 1: MULTIPLE CHOICE OPTIONS

Test 1: The Restless Earth   8
Test 2: Treasure Island   10
Test 3: Pinocchio   12
Test 4: Trains   14
Test 5: The Butterfly Lion   16
Billy's Fun Vocabulary Page: Helpful Homophones   18
Test 6: The Adventures of Maya the Bee   19
Test 7: Indira's Pets   22
Test 8: The Story of Dr Dolittle   25
Test 9: The Fir Tree   28
Test 10: The Phoenix and the Carpet   31
Billy's Fun Vocabulary Page: Tricky Tenses   35

SECTION 2: PARTIAL WORDS

Test 11: The Planets   38
Test 12: David Copperfield   40
Test 13: Peter Pan   42
Test 14: My First Day at School   44
Test 15: War Horse   46
Billy's Fun Vocabulary Page: Super Synonyms   47
Test 16: The Adventures of Tom Sawyer   48
Test 17: The Jungle Book   50
Test 18: The Frog Prince   52
Test 19: Rebecca of Sunnybrook Farm   54
Test 20: The Velveteen Rabbit   56
Billy's Fun Vocabulary Page: Strenuous Spellings   58

SECTION 3: WORD BANKS

Test 21: The Railway Children   60
Test 22: The Wonderful City of Oz   62
Test 23: Deep Sea Wildlife   64
Test 24: Australia   65
Test 25: White Fang   66
Billy's Fun Vocabulary Page: Awesome Antonyms   68
Test 26: The Selfish Giant   70
Test 27: Heidi   72
Test 28: Robin Hood   74
Test 29: The Secret Garden   76
Test 30: The Elephant's Child   78
Billy's Fun Vocabulary Page: Awesome Adjectives   80

Contents

SECTION 4: MIXED CLOZE PASSAGES

Test 31: A Christmas Carol — 82
Test 32: The Wind in the Willows — 85
Test 33: Flowers and Herbs — 86
Test 34: The Day of the Exam — 88
Test 35: Gulliver's Travels — 90
Billy's Fun Vocabulary Page: Perfect Plurals 1 — 92
Test 36: The Emperor's New Clothes — 93
Test 37: Just William — 96
Test 38: The Railway Children — 98
Test 39: The Book of Dragons — 100
Test 40: Tom Brown's School Days — 102
Billy's Fun Vocabulary Page: Perfect Plurals 2 — 105

SECTION 5: GLOSSARY AND ANSWERS

Glossary — 107
Multiple Choice Options (tests 1–5) — 109
Multiple Choice Options (tests 6–10) — 110
Partial Words (tests 11–15) — 111
Partial Words (tests 16–20) — 112
Word Banks (tests 21–25) — 113
Word Banks (tests 26–30) — 114
Mixed Cloze Passages (tests 31–35) — 115
Mixed Cloze Passages (tests 36–40) — 116
Billy's Fun Vocabulary Pages — 117

Marking Chart — **119**
Progress Grid — **120**

Introduction

Teachitright

This book has been published in collaboration with Teachitright, one of the most successful 11+ tuition companies in the South-East. It has supported thousands of pupils for both grammar school and independent school entry. Teachitright has several tuition centres across the UK, including Berkshire, Buckinghamshire and West Midlands.

With considerable experience and knowledge, Teachitright has produced a range of books to support children through their 11+ journey for both CEM style and many Common Entrance exams. The books have been written by qualified teachers, tested in the classroom with pupils, and adapted to ensure children are fully prepared and able to perform to the best of their ability.

Teachitright's unique mascot, Billy, helps to guide children through the book and gives helpful hints and tips along the way. We hope your child finds this book useful and informative and we wish them luck on their 11+ journey.

Teachitright hold a number of comprehensive revision courses and mock exams throughout the year. For more information, visit www.teachitright.com

Introduction

Importance of Cloze Tests

Cloze tests are passages which have omitted words. They appear in 11+ and Common Entrance exams so it is important to practise these types of questions. They can be presented in different formats:

1. Multiple Choice: In this version of Cloze passages, the words are presented in a multiple choice format. Three words are given for each question and only one word will correctly complete the passage.

2. Partial Words: In a given passage, some of the words have letters removed which need to be filled in correctly. The importance of good spelling skills are tested in this element of Cloze tests.

3. Word Banks: The words required to complete the passage are provided and the pupil must choose the correct word from the bank.

In this book, there are both classic and contemporary texts. The carefully selected texts include extracts from world-renowned authors such as Michael Morpurgo's *War Horse* and *The Butterfly Lion*.

How to use this book

This book provides exercises to practise authentic Cloze passages, written by experts, under timed conditions. After each test, the pupil should mark their work and look up any words they do not know and record them. This will aid learning and revision of new words. It is also important to try and finish the passages in the recommended timings.

The results grid at the back gives the perfect opportunity to record progress. Each section equates to 100 words. A supportive set of statements guides pupils on to next steps and there is a glossary for key words.

Online video tutorial

An online video tutorial to help with techniques is available at:
www.collins.co.uk/11plusresources

SECTION I:
MULTIPLE CHOICE OPTIONS

Look out for Billy's tips and hints.

1. THE RESTLESS EARTH

 06:00
06 minutes

Mark the box with a pencil line next to the correct word to complete the sentence. ⊏═══⊐

What causes earthquakes and volcanoes to shake (1.)
☐ a. are
☐ b. our   planet? This
☐ c. hour

passage examines why some of these phenomena occur. Terra firma is a Latin

☐ a. phrase
(2.) ☐ b. phase   meaning firm, or solid, ground. It is what people call the land we
☐ c. telling

☐ a. walked   ☐ a. learn,
(3.) ☐ b. walk   upon. It is surprising to (4.) ☐ b. lean,   therefore, that once
☐ c. walking   ☐ c. knew,

every thirty seconds somewhere in the world, the earth shakes a little! Usually,

☐ a. this
(5.) ☐ b. these   tremors are too small to be felt, but every few months the
☐ c. those

☐ a. Earth's
(6.) ☐ b. Earths   crust shifts significantly, often with catastrophic results.
☐ c. earth's

☐ a. Scientists
What causes the Earth to move in such a restless way? (7.) ☐ b. scientist's   in the
☐ c. Scientist's

☐ a. had
fascinating field of Plate Tectonics (8.) ☐ b. having   some of the answers. They have
☐ c. have

studied the eight major tectonic plates of the Earth's crust which float on top of the

☐ a. lie
molten mantle which (9.) ☐ b. lay   beneath the surface of our planet and its
☐ c. lies

1. THE RESTLESS EARTH (CONT.)

core. As plates move very slowly, they try to slide past each other at places called fault

[ ] a. below

lines – such as the one at San Andreas, California. The pressure (10.) [ ] b. between

[ ] c. outside

these plates (11.)
[ ] a. billed
[ ] b. builds up until suddenly they (12.)
[ ] c. bills

[ ] a. slips
[ ] b. slipping   and lurch
[ ] c. slip

past each other, making the land shake (13.)
[ ] a. on
[ ] b. above   a devastating earthquake
[ ] c. in

which can (14.)
[ ] a. brings
[ ] b. bringing   down buildings. If it occurs on the seabed, this quake
[ ] c. bring

can cause a tidal wave to sweep over the land, destroying everything in (15.)
[ ] a. it's
[ ] b. it
[ ] c. its

path. When plates slip beneath each other, subduction zones (16.)
[ ] a. is
[ ] b. are   created.
[ ] c. our

(17.)
[ ] a. Here,
[ ] b. Hear,   material from the Earth's crust is thrust into the mantle
[ ] c. There,

(18.)
[ ] a. so
[ ] b. and rises up under great pressure, exploding (19.)
[ ] c. but

[ ] a. into
[ ] b. onto   the
[ ] c. under

surface as a magnificent but terrifying volcano, such as Mount St. Helens in the USA or

Vesuvius in Italy, which (20.)
[ ] a. buried
[ ] b. berried   the ancient Roman city of Pompeii in AD 79.
[ ] c. bury

2. TREASURE ISLAND
By Robert Louis Stevenson

Mark the box with a pencil line next to the correct word to complete the sentence.

The old seadog had taken me (1.)
- a. beside
- b. aside
- c. inside

one day and (2.)
- a. promised
- b. predicted
- c. paid

a silver fourpenny on the first of every month if only I would keep my "weather eye open

for a (3.)
- a. seafaring
- b. seaman
- c. seaworthy

man with one leg" and let him know the moment he appeared.

Often enough when the first of the month came round and I (4.)
- a. appealed
- b. applied
- c. appalled

for

my (5.)
- a. wage
- b. wager
- c. pension

he would only blow (6.)
- a. through
- b. thought his nose at me
- c. threw

and stare me down, but before the week was out he (7.)
- a. is
- b. was
- c. were

sure to think better

of it, bring me my fourpenny piece, and (8.)
- a. request
- b. repeat
- c. repeal

his orders to look out for "the

seafaring man with one leg." How that (9.)
- a. personage
- b. populace
- c. apparition

haunted my dreams I

need (10.)
- a. scared
- b. scarcely
- c. scarily

tell you. On (11.)
- a. stormy
- b. calm
- c. Saturday

nights when the

wind shook the four corners of the house and the surf roared along the (12.)
- a. cove
- b. cave
- c. ridge

2. TREASURE ISLAND (CONT.)

and up the cliffs, I (13.) ☐ a. will
☐ b. would   see him in a thousand forms, and with a
☐ c. won't

thousand diabolical (14.) ☐ a. expires.
☐ b. expressions.   Now the leg would be cut off at the
☐ c. expressives.

knee, now at the hip; (15.) ☐ a. now
☐ b. were   he was a monstrous kind of creature who
☐ c. wore

(16.) ☐ a. hadn't
☐ b. had   never had but the one leg, and that in the middle of his body. To
☐ c. have

see him leap and run and pursue me over hedge and ditch was the worst of

(17.) ☐ a. thoughts.
☐ b. dreams.   And altogether I paid pretty (18.) ☐ a. dire
☐ c. nightmares.   ☐ b. dear   for my
☐ c. deer

(19.) ☐ a. annual
☐ b. monthly   fourpenny piece, in the shape of these
☐ c. weekly

abominable (20.) ☐ a. fantastic.
☐ b. fantasy.
☐ c. fancies.

Remember to refer to the whole of the text and not just that one sentence for relevant facts that may help you to answer the questions.

3. PINOCCHIO

Mark the box with a pencil line next to the correct word to complete the sentence.

a. stupidly

But Pinocchio was (1.) b. stubborn as ever.

c. stopped

a. week."

"Are you deaf? Wait young man we will get it from you in a (2.) b. twinkling."

c. fighting."

a. desperation

In (3.) b. despairing the smaller of the two assassins pulled out a long knife from

c. decision

a. pry

his pocket and tried to (4.) b. prize Pinocchio's mouth open with it. Quick as a

c. put

a. hardly

flash the marionette sank his teeth (5.) b. deep into the assassin's hand, bit it

c. carefully

a. spat

off and (6.) b. spits it out. Fancy his surprise when he saw it was not a hand but

c. spatted

a. them

a cat's paw. Encouraged by this first victory, he freed (7.) b. it from the

c. himself

a. leaped

claws of his assailers and (8.) b. leaping over the bushes along the road, ran

c. leapt

a. swiftly   a. chaste

(9.) b. slowly across the fields. His (10.) b. pursuers were after him at once

c. tearing   c. men

like two dogs chasing a hare. After running seven miles or so, Pinocchio was well-nigh

3. PINOCCHIO (CONT.)

a. exhausted.

(11.) b. happy.   Seeing himself lost, he climbed an (12.)

a. tallest

b. enormous

c. gone.

c. giant

a. will

pine tree and sat there to see what he (13.) b. can   see. The assassins tried to

c. could

a. dropped.

climb also, but they slipped and (14.) b. fell.   Far from (15.)

a. stopping

b. giving

c. hurt.

c. stepping

up the chase, this only spurred them on. They gathered a bundle of wood,

a. pilled

(16.) b. piled   it up at the foot of the pine, and set fire to it. In a twinkling the

c. piling

a. began

tree (17.) b. begins   to sputter and burn like a candle in the wind. Pinocchio saw

c. starts

a. higher

the flames climb (18.) b. above   and higher. Not wishing to end his days as a

c. bright

a. feet

roasted marionette, he jumped quickly to the (19.) b. bottom   and off he went,

c. ground

the assassins close to him as before.

a. warning

Dawn was breaking when, without any (20.) b. looking   whatsoever, Pinocchio saw

c. chance

his path barred by a deep pool of water the colour of muddy coffee. What was there to

do? With a "One, two, three!" he jumped clear across it.

4. TRAINS

 06:00
06 minutes

Mark the box with a pencil line next to the correct word to complete the sentence.

Trains were (1.)
☐ a. build
☐ b. assemble   more than 200 years ago. Many people felt they
☐ c. built

were the most wonderful of all (2.)
☐ a. inventions.
☐ b. inventors.   Nonetheless, others felt
☐ c. inventive.

smoking steam engines (3.)
☐ a. were
☐ b. was   like ugly metal monsters.
☐ c. is

Trains certainly changed the world. Over the years, this (4.)
☐ a. investable
☐ b. incredible
☐ c. inseparable

invention changed the way we travelled on a daily basis and its engineering

(5.)
☐ a. building
☐ b. industry   has continually (6.)
☐ c. technology

☐ a. increased.
☐ b. developed.   People and goods could
☐ c. distanced

be carried long distances in vast (7.)
☐ a. quantities.
☐ b. quantity.   Distant lands became almost
☐ c. distanced.

instantly (8.)
☐ a. reaching,
☐ b. reachable,   for example, the journey between New York and
☐ c. far,

California was (9.)
☐ a. condensed
☐ b. contained   from two months to a few days! Trains are
☐ c. decrease

(10.)
☐ a. deferential
☐ b. deficiency an (11.)
☐ c. definitely

☐ a. efficient
☐ b. effluent   method of transport. They use less
☐ c. ineffective

4. TRAINS (CONT.)

☐ a. produce

fuel and (12.) ☐ b. productive   less pollution than cars. Today they still transport

☐ c. producer

☐ a. trains.

around 40% of the world's (13.) ☐ b. weight.

☐ c. cargo.

☐ a. approached

The first steam train (14.) ☐ b. appeared   in England in the early 18th century.

☐ c. approach

☐ a. kilometres

Now England has over 15,000 (15.) ☐ b. meters   of working railways, with

☐ c. long

14,353 used for passenger trains. Within the rail network there are over 40,000 bridges

☐ a. roads.   ☐ a. underground

and (16.) ☐ b. rivers.   The first (17.) ☐ b. overground   railway was created

☐ c. tunnels.   ☐ c. flat

☐ a. links

in London. Although this small (18.) ☐ b. network   of tunnels had problems with

☐ c. webs

☐ a. wasted

steam engine smoke, its popularity never (19.) ☐ b. wavered   and is still used today.

☐ c. wondered

One of the most world-famous railway lines is the Trans-Siberian Express which

☐ a. connected

(20.) ☐ b. merges   Moscow and Vladivostok. It is 9297 kilometres long.

☐ c. connects

5. THE BUTTERFLY LION
By Michael Morpurgo

06:00
06 minutes

Mark the box with a pencil line next to the correct word to complete the sentence.

I was still (1.) ☐ a. deciding ☐ b. decided ☐ c. decisive which direction to take when I (2.) ☐ a. hearing ☐ b. heard ☐ c. herd a voice from

behind me. "Who are you? What do you want?" "Who are you?" she asked (3.) ☐ a. now. ☐ b. again. ☐ c. them.

The old lady who (4.) ☐ a. stands ☐ b. stood ☐ c. stand before me was no bigger than I was. She

(5.) ☐ a. scrutinised ☐ b. scrimmaged ☐ c. scrounged me from under the shadow of her dripping straw hat. She had

(6.) ☐ a. pining ☐ b. pinching ☐ c. piercing dark eyes that I did not want to look into. "I didn't think it would

(7.) ☐ a. rain," ☐ b. rein," ☐ c. reign," she said, her voice (8.) ☐ a. geniune. ☐ b. gentler. ☐ c. gentlest. "Lost are you?" I said nothing.

She had a dog on a (9.) ☐ a. leash ☐ b. lease ☐ c. leech at her side, a big dog. There was an (10.) ☐ a. ominous ☐ b. nervous ☐ c. playful

growl in his throat, and his (11.) ☐ a. hysteria ☐ b. haggled ☐ c. hackles were up all along his back. She smiled. "The dog

says (12.) ☐ a. your ☐ b. you're ☐ c. yours on private (13.) ☐ a. property," ☐ b. prosperity," ☐ c. prospectus," she went on, pointing her

5. THE BUTTERFLY LION (CONT.)

stick at me (14.)
- [ ] a. accusingly
- [ ] b. accordingly.
- [ ] c. acceptably

She edged (15.)
- [ ] a. awhile
- [ ] b. aside
- [ ] c. along

my raincoat with the

end of her stick. "Run away from that school, did you? Well, if it's (16.)
- [ ] a. anything
- [ ] b. nothing
- [ ] c. everything

like it used (17.)
- [ ] a. to
- [ ] b. two
- [ ] c. too

be, I (18.)
- [ ] a. can't
- [ ] b. could
- [ ] c. can

say I blame you. But we can't

just (19.)
- [ ] a. stood
- [ ] b. wonder
- [ ] c. stand

here in the rain, can we? You'd better come inside.

(20.)
- [ ] a. We'll
- [ ] b. We'd
- [ ] c. We've

give him some tea, shall we, Jack? Don't you worry about Jack.

He's all bark and no bite." Looking at Jack, I found that hard to believe.

Remember that the tense of the verbs in the passage should agree.

HELPFUL HOMOPHONES

Can you help Billy by writing down a homophone partner to the words below?

1. hour ....

2. in ....

3. here ....

4. through ....

5. would ....

6. dear ....

7. passed ....

8. beat ....

9. bury ....

10. profit ....

Homophones are words that sound the same but have different spellings and meaning.

Teachitright Teaser: Select two pairs of homophones from the list above and put them into sentences of your own. See if you can be really clever and include a pair of homophones in the same sentence!

1.

2.

6. THE ADVENTURES OF MAYA THE BEE 05:00 05 minutes

By Waldemar Bonsels

Mark the box with a pencil line next to the correct word to complete the sentence. ⊏━━━⊐

Maya, a young bee, has set out alone into the world in the search of adventure. Bobbie has met a rather arrogant and vain dung beetle whom she decides to tease a little. As a result of this he falls.

⊏━⊐ a. when

Bobbie had hardly uttered the last word (1.) ⊏━⊐ b. after   something dreadful

⊏━⊐ c. so

⊏━⊐ a. disappear

happened. In his eagerness to (2.) ⊏━⊐ b. appear   indifferent, he had lost his balance

⊏━⊐ c. show

⊏━⊐ a. trees   ⊏━⊐ a. shriek

and toppled (3.) ⊏━⊐ b. over. Maya heard a despairing (4.) ⊏━⊐ b. whisper,   and the

⊏━⊐ c. up   ⊏━⊐ c. shouting

⊏━⊐ a. his

next instant saw the beetle lying flat on (5.) ⊏━⊐ b. her   back in the grass, his arms

⊏━⊐ c. their

and legs waving pitifully in the air.

⊏━⊐ a. doing

"I'm (6.) ⊏━⊐ b. did   for," he wailed. I can't get back on my feet again. I'll

⊏━⊐ c. done

⊏━⊐ a. never

(7.) ⊏━⊐ b. possibly   be able to get back on my feet again. I'll die.

⊏━⊐ c. surely

⊏━⊐ a. fare

I'll die in this position. Have you ever heard of a worse (8.) ⊏━⊐ b. fate   !"

⊏━⊐ c. fete

⊏━⊐ a. comfort

He carried on so that he did not hear Maya trying to (9.) ⊏━⊐ b. cuddle   him.

⊏━⊐ c. catch

(continued over)

6. THE ADVENTURES OF MAYA THE BEE (CONT.)

He kept making efforts to touch the ground with his feet. (10.)
☐ a. Each
☐ b. In   time he'd
☐ c. On

painfully get hold of a bit of earth, it would give way, and he'd fall over again on his high

half-sphere of a (11.)
☐ a. back
☐ b. tummy.   The case looked really desperate, and Maya was
☐ c. head

(12.)
☐ a. hardly
☐ b. honestly   concerned; he was already quite pale in the face and his cries were
☐ c. not

heart-rending. "I can't stand (13.)
☐ a. it
☐ b. these   , I can't stand this position," he yelled.
☐ c. by

"At least turn your head away. Don't torture a dying man with your inquisitive

(14.)
☐ a. stairs.
☐ b. stares.   If only I could reach a (15.)
☐ c. stars.

☐ a. flower
☐ b. blade   of grass or the stem of
☐ c. petal

the buttercup. You (16.)
☐ a. could
☐ b. can   hold on to the air. Nobody can do that. Nobody
☐ c. can't

can hold on to the air."

Maya's heart (17.)
☐ a. is
☐ b. begun   quivering with pity.
☐ c. was

"Wait," she cried, "I'll try to turn you over. If I try very hard I am (18.)
☐ a. bound
☐ b. knotted   to
☐ c. tied

succeed. But Bobbie, Bobbie, dear man, don't yell like that. Listen to me. If I

6. THE ADVENTURES OF MAYA THE BEE (CONT.)

☐ a. break

(19.) ☐ b. blow a blade of grass over and reach the tip of it to you, will you be able

☐ c. bend

to use it and save yourself?"

☐ a. Afraid

Bobbie had no ears for her suggestion. (20.) ☐ b. Frightened out of his senses, he did

☐ c. Feared

nothing but kick and scream.

So little Maya, in spite of the rain, flew out of her cover over to a slim green blade of grass beside Bobbie, and clung to it near the tip. It bent under her weight and sank directly above Bobbie's wriggling limbs. Maya gave a little cry of delight.

"Catch hold of it!" she called.

Before you attempt the answers, read right through the passage. This will give you an overview of its content and help you to establish whether the characters are male or female, and which tense the passage is written in. Many of the questions will require an understanding of these.

7. INDIRA'S PETS

Mark the box with a pencil line next to the correct word to complete the sentence.

In the following extract, a little girl called Indira has good intentions, but her overenthusiastic care for her pet fish has disastrous consequences.

Indira loved (1.)
- a. some
- b. all
- c. most

of her pets with a passion; none was more special than

another and she (2.)
- a. prided
- b. played
- c. proved

herself on her conscientious (3.)
- a. attention
- b. attending
- c. attentive

to their needs. Her latest acquisition was a beautiful golden fish who delighted her because

he never seemed to (4.)
- a. tyre
- b. tire
- c. tier

of listening to her. Regardless of

(5.)
- a. whenever
- b. whoever
- c. however

long she took to share the trials and tribulations of her life, he

always paced (6.)
- a. along
- b. through
- c. around

his bowl, giving careful consideration to her woes and

responding as he passed with a wide-mouthed, sympathetic, "Oh!"

Flippy was aptly named, as (7.)
- a. its
- b. her tail
- c. his

flickered with joy every time he saw

her. He was "practically perfect in every way" except for one defect which constantly

(8.)
- a. viewed
- b. vexed
- c. varied

her. The large black spot on his back seemed to Indira to be

7. INDIRA'S PETS (CONT.)

condemnatory evidence of her failure to keep him (9.)
- a. quiet
- b. still . The fault was not
- c. clean

entirely (10.)
- a. hers
- b. true . She had noticed the offending mark in the pet shop
- c. certain

and had considered admonishing the lady for her neglect (11.)
- a. but
- b. she had
- c. consequently

decided that the unfortunate fish would (12.)
- a. fur
- b. fare better in her own assiduous care.
- c. fear

One (13.)
- a. fateful
- b. morning day, Indira decided that she must deal with the offending
- c. Sunday

spot. She waited patiently for a moment when Flippy appeared more than usually

somnolent, and stealthily (14.)
- a. looked
- b. went into his domain with a loving hand.
- c. reached

There was a little resistance, understandable considering her failure to

(15.)
- a. notify
- b. ask him of her benevolent intent, but after a short chase she triumphantly
- c. know

extracted him from his bowl. He was clearly delighted with his unexpected freedom, for

his (16.)
- a. tale
- b. legs flipped so violently from one side to (17.)
- c. tail

- a. other
- b. side that he
- c. another

would have been a serious contender in a goldfish Olympics. His eyes bulged wide with

awe and wonder of the new world (18.)
- a. that
- b. were he found himself in, and he
- c. what

gasped with joy. Without further ado, Indira set about the task with

(continued over)

7. INDIRA'S PETS (CONT.)

      ☐ a. enthusiastic

(19.) ☐ b. soap   and (fearing a flannel to be too harsh) cotton wool. Flippy lay

      ☐ c. help

passive and unresisting, clearly relaxed, blissfully grateful for Indira's kind and loving

      ☐ a. helping

(20.) ☐ b. girl   .

      ☐ c. ministrations

If you are not sure which word to choose, read ahead to see how the sentence ends. This will help you to understand the word in context and help you find the one that makes sense.

8. THE STORY OF DR DOLITTLE
by Hugh Lofting

Mark the box with a pencil line next to the correct word to complete the sentence. ⬜

Dr Dolittle is a vet who can talk to the animals. In this extract, he and his animal friends are on a voyage across the sea to Africa.

⬜ a. hole

Now for six (1.) ⬜ b. whole   weeks they went sailing on and on, over the rolling

⬜ c. while

⬜ a. sea   ⬜ a. car

(2.) ⬜ b. river, following the swallow who flew before the (3.) ⬜ b. ship to show

⬜ c. ice   ⬜ c. start

⬜ a. carries

them the way. At night she (4.) ⬜ b. carrying a tiny lantern, so they should not miss

⬜ c. carried

her in the dark; and the people on the other ships that passed said that the light must

⬜ a. shooting

be a (5.) ⬜ b. shot   star.

⬜ c. chuting

⬜ a. sales

As they (6.) ⬜ b. sailed further and further into the South, it got warmer and

⬜ c. sailing

⬜ a. warm

(7.) ⬜ b. warmer . Polynesia, Chee-Chee and the crocodile enjoyed the hot sun no

⬜ c. warmest

end. They ran about laughing and looking over the side of the ship to

⬜ a. sea

(8.) ⬜ b. seeing   if they could see Africa yet.

⬜ c. see

(continued over)

8. THE STORY OF DR DOLITTLE (CONT.)

But the pig and the dog and the owl, Too-Too, could do nothing in such weather, but sat

at the end of the ship in the (9.)
- a. brightness
- b. shade   of a big barrel, with
- c. light

(10.)
- a. there
- b. they're   tongues hanging out, drinking lemonade.
- c. their

Dab-Dab, the duck, used to keep herself cool by jumping into the sea and

(11.)
- a. swim
- b. swimming   behind the ship. And every once in a while, when the top of
- c. swimmer

her head got (12.)
- a. to
- b. two   hot, she would dive (13.)
- c. too

- a. over
- b. under   the ship and
- c. up

come up on the other side. In this way, too, she used to catch herrings on Tuesdays and

Fridays—when everybody on the (14.)
- a. bowl
- b. boat   ate fish to make the beef last longer.
- c. bout

When they got near to the Equator they (15.)
- a. seed
- b. saw   some flying-fishes
- c. sore

(16.)
- a. came
- b. coming   towards them. And the fishes asked the parrot if this was Doctor
- c. come

Dolittle's ship. When she (17.)
- a. told
- b. tolled   them it was, they said they
- c. telled

(18.)
- a. were
- b. where   glad, because the (19.)
- c. are

- a. monkey
- b. monkeys   in Africa were getting
- c. monies

8. THE STORY OF DR DOLITTLE (CONT.)

worried that he (20.)

☐ a. wood

☐ b. wouldn't   never come. Polynesia asked them how many

☐ c. would

miles they had yet to go; and the flying-fishes said it was only fifty-five miles now to the coast of Africa.

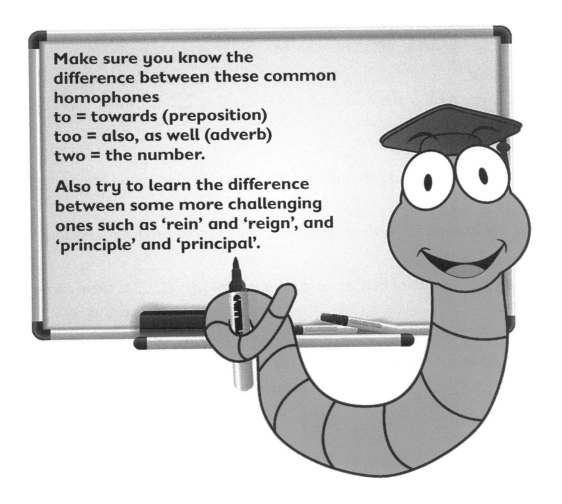

Make sure you know the difference between these common homophones
to = towards (preposition)
too = also, as well (adverb)
two = the number.

Also try to learn the difference between some more challenging ones such as 'rein' and 'reign', and 'principle' and 'principal'.

9. THE FIR TREE
By Hans Christian Andersen

05:00
05 minutes

Mark the box with a pencil line next to the correct word to complete the sentence.

In this extract, a young fir tree longs to grow tall. This overwhelming desire makes him discontent, unaware and unappreciative of all that surrounds him.

a. stands

Out in the woods (1.) b. standing   a nice little Fir Tree. The place he had was a very

c. stood

a. one   a. him

good (2.) b. time : the sun shone on (3.) b. her and, as to fresh air, there was

c. thing   c. it

a. on

enough of that and (4.) b. up   him grew many large-sized comrades, pines as

c. around

a. wants

well as firs. But the little Fir (5.) b. wanting so very much to be a grown-up tree.

c. wanted

a. don't   a. sparkling

He (6.) b. isn't   think of the warm sun and of the (7.) b. fresh   air; he did

c. didn't   c. night

a. up

not care for the little cottage children that ran (8.) b. about and prattled when they

c. down

were in the woods looking for wild strawberries. The children often came with a

a. howl   a. they

(9.) b. hole   pitcher full of berries, or a long row of (10.) b. them threaded on

c. whole   c. that

a. young

a straw, and sat down near the (11.) b. old   tree and said, "Oh, how pretty he

c. ancient

9. THE FIR TREE (CONT.)

is! What a nice little fir!" But this was what the Tree could not (12.)
- [ ] a. bare
- [ ] b. bear to hear.
- [ ] c. bere

At the end of a year he had (13.)
- [ ] a. shot
- [ ] b. grew up a good deal, and after
- [ ] c. gone

another year he was (14.)
- [ ] a. again
- [ ] b. about   long bit taller; for with fir trees one can
- [ ] c. another

always tell by the shoots how many years old they are.

"Oh! (15.)
- [ ] a. Where
- [ ] b. Were   I but such a high tree as the others are," sighed he. "Then I
- [ ] c. Whirr

should be (16.)
- [ ] a. possible
- [ ] b. going   to spread out my branches, and with the tops to
- [ ] c. able

look into the wide world! Then would the birds build nests among my branches: and

when there was a (17.)
- [ ] a. breeze
- [ ] b. windy   , I could bend with as much stateliness as the
- [ ] c. rainy

others!" Neither the sunbeams, nor the birds, nor the red clouds which morning and

evening (18.)
- [ ] a. spoke
- [ ] b. sailed   above him, gave the little Tree any pleasure.
- [ ] c. twittered

In winter, when the snow lay glittering on the ground, a hare would often come leaping

along, and jump right over the little Tree. Oh, that made him so (19.)
- [ ] a. angry
- [ ] b. happy   !
- [ ] c. surprised

But two winters were past, and in the third the Tree was so large that the hare was

(continued over)

9. THE FIR TREE (CONT.)

obliged to go round it. "To grow and grow, to get older and be tall," thought the Tree —

a. frightening

"that, after all, is the most (20.) ☐ b. nicest   thing in the world!"

c. delightful

In autumn the wood-cutters always came and felled some of the largest trees. This happened every year; and the young Fir Tree, that had now grown to a very comely size, trembled at the sight; for the magnificent great trees fell to the earth with noise and cracking, the branches were lopped off, and the trees looked long and bare; they were hardly to be recognised; and then they were laid in carts, and the horses dragged them out of the wood.

Where did they go to?

What became of them?

As you read the passage, notice who it is about — even trees can have characters and feelings! Are they enthusiastic, unhappy, or hopeful and expectant like this little fir? Understanding characterisation will help you choose the right word to complete sentences about emotions.

10. THE PHOENIX AND THE CARPET
05:00 05 minutes
By Edith Nesbit

Mark the box with a pencil line next to the correct word to complete the sentence.

In this extract, some children are watching a strange and magical egg which is lying amid the heat and flames of their living room fire.

"Oh, stop," cried Anthea. "Look at it! Look! Look! Look! I do believe

a. someone
(1.) b. something IS going to happen!"
c. nothing

For the egg was now red-hot, and inside it something was moving. Next moment

a. they're
(2.) b. there   was a soft (3.)
c. their

a. cracking
b. crunching sound; the egg burst in
c. crumbling

a. to
(4.) b. too , and out of it came a flame-coloured bird. It rested a moment among
c. two

a. four
the flames, and as it rested there the (5.) b. for   children could see it growing
c. fore

bigger and bigger under their eyes.

a. ear
Every (6.) b. nose   was a-gape, every eye a-goggle.
c. mouth

a. rose
The bird (7.) b. rise   in its nest of fire, stretched its wings, and flew out into the
c. risen

(continued over)

10. THE PHOENIX AND THE CARPET (CONT.)

room. It flew round and round, and round again, and where it passed the air was

(8.) ☐ a. worn.
☐ b. warm. Then it perched on the fender. The children (9.) ☐ a. looked
☐ c. worm.
☐ b. looking at
☐ c. look

each other. Then Cyril put out a hand towards the bird. It put its head on one side and

☐ a. may
looked up at him, as you (10.) ☐ b. made have seen a parrot do when it is just
☐ c. May

☐ a. went
(11.) ☐ b. gone to speak, so that the children were hardly astonished at all when it
☐ c. going

said, "Be careful; I am not nearly cool yet."

They were not astonished, but they were very, very much interested.

☐ a. feathers
They looked at the bird, and it was certainly worth looking at. Its (12.) ☐ b. beak
☐ c. head

were like gold. It was about as large as a bantam, only its beak was not at all

bantam-shaped. "I believe I know what it is," said Robert. "I've seen a picture."

☐ a. crawl
He (13.) ☐ b. hurry   away. A hasty dash and scramble among the papers on Father's
☐ c. hurried

10. THE PHOENIX AND THE CARPET (CONT.)

study table yielded, as the sum-books say, "the desired result". But when he

(14.)
- [ ] a. coming
- [ ] b. came back into the room holding out a paper, and crying, "I say, look
- [ ] c. go

here," the (15.)
- [ ] a. others
- [ ] b. adults all said "Hush!" and he hushed obediently and instantly,
- [ ] c. birds

(16.)
- [ ] a. four
- [ ] b. for the bird was speaking.
- [ ] c. five

"Which of you," it was (17.)
- [ ] a. said
- [ ] b. speak , "put the egg into the fire?"
- [ ] c. saying

"He did," said three voices, and three fingers pointed at Robert.

The bird bowed; at (18.)
- [ ] a. least
- [ ] b. less it was more like that than anything else.
- [ ] c. last

"I am your grateful debtor," it said with a high-bred air.

The children were all choking with wonder and curiosity — all except Robert. He held

the paper in his hand, and he KNEW. He said so. He said —

"I (19.)
- [ ] a. no
- [ ] b. now who you are."
- [ ] c. know

(continued over)

10. THE PHOENIX AND THE CARPET (CONT.)

And he opened and displayed a printed paper, at the head of (20.)

☐ a. witch
☐ b. which was a
☐ c. watch

little picture of a bird sitting in a nest of flames.

"You are the Phoenix," said Robert; and the bird was quite pleased.

Some important homophones you need to know are:
there: over there (adverb);
their: their (belonging to them, possessive determiner);
they're: they are (contraction of 'they' and 'are').

TRICKY TENSES

In multiple-choice Cloze passages, you must consider the tense the extract is written in. This will help when selecting the words to keep the tense consistent.

Verb tenses are important, as they tell us when an action has taken place – present, past and future.

The past tense of irregular verbs can be a bit tricky as you will need to do more than simply adding 'd' or 'ed' to the end of the root word. You will need to memorise these spellings. The **past participle** of a verb is a form that is usually the same as the past form and so ends in 'ed'. However, several verbs have irregular past participles. For example, the past participle for *break* is *broken*.

Try to complete the table below with the correct irregular verbs.

	Present tense	Past tense	Past participle
1		flew	flown
2	buy		bought
3	blow	blew	
4		brought	brought
5	break		broken
6	bite	bit	
7		built	built
8	catch		caught
9	drink	drank	
10		drew	drawn

Check at the back of the book to see how many you have correct.

A verb's tense is determined by when the action takes place, which could be in the present, past or future.

THIS PAGE HAS DELIBERATELY BEEN LEFT BLANK

SECTION 2:
PARTIAL WORDS

11. THE PLANETS

08:00
08 minutes

Fill in the missing letters to complete the words in the following passage.

I (1.) w⬜nd⬜r if you know that scientists (2.) s⬜m⬜ti⬜⬜s call Earth the Goldilocks planet. Can you (3.) g⬜⬜ss why? It is because it is the only planet in our solar system that can (4.) s⬜st⬜⬜n life.

It is (5.) n⬜⬜the⬜ too wet nor dry, too hot nor cold, and therefore its conditions are "just right" for living (6.) c⬜⬜atu⬜es.

A planet is defined as "a large round object in space that moves around a star such as the Sun, and (7.) r⬜c⬜ive⬜ light from it." The Earth is one of a family of eight planets in our solar system and they are all different (8.) f⬜⬜m each other in many respects, such as size shape and conditions. Jupiter is the (9.) ⬜⬜rge⬜⬜ and coldest, Mercury the smallest, and Venus the hottest. The distances between them are (10.) ⬜n⬜⬜mo⬜s.

A moon is a smaller object that can be found orbiting a planet. Some planets have many moons orbiting (11.) ⬜r⬜⬜nd them but Earth has only one, called "The Moon". A star is a huge (12.) l⬜min⬜⬜s ball composed of very hot gases; it gives out lots of light and heat. Some stars have planets (13.) ⬜ircl⬜⬜g around them but not all do. The collective noun for a group of stars is a galaxy. The galaxy in which our planet Earth circles its star, the Sun, is (14.) c⬜l⬜ed the Milky Way. There are at least 146 moons circling in our Milky Way.

I wonder which is your (15.) fa⬜o⬜⬜ite planet? Mine is Saturn because of the (16.) s⬜u⬜⬜ing beauty of its ring system. It is surrounded by eighteen rings which are made of billions of particles of ice and rock. Jupiter

II. THE PLANETS (CONT.)

is also amazing. It is a massive liquid planet made mostly of hydrogen and helium and it is (17.) **su**☐☐**ou**☐☐**ed** by gases and clouds. How (18.) **a**☐**e**☐**ome** to think that 1,321 Earths could fit into Jupiter.

Pluto has the saddest story of all, I think. It used to be considered the ninth planet in our solar system but (19.) **s**☐☐**l**☐, scientists decided that it no longer fitted the criteria of a planet. It is now known as a Dwarf Planet.

The planets have always been an endless source of (20.) **fa**☐☐**in**☐☐**ion** to mankind. As science progresses and our knowledge expands, we realise that there is so much more that we do not know or understand. Thus, even more they become objects of awe and wonder for us.

12. DAVID COPPERFIELD
By Charles Dickens

Fill in the missing letters to complete the words in the following passage.

I had led this life about a month, when I was (1.) i☐f☐r☐☐☐ by Mr Mell that Mr Creakle would be home that (2.) **ev**☐☐**i**☐☐. In the evening, after tea, I heard that he was come. Before bedtime, I was (3.) **fe**☐☐**he**☐ to appear before him.

Mr Creakle's part of the house was a good deal more (4.) **co**☐☐**or**☐**a**☐☐☐ than ours. I went on my way, trembling, to Mr Creakle's (5.) ☐**re**☐☐**nce**: which so abashed me, that I hardly saw Mrs Creakle or Miss Creakle (who were both there in the parlour) or anything but Mr Creakle, a (6.) **s**☐☐**ut** gentleman with a bunch of watch-chain and seals in an arm-(7.) ☐☐☐☐☐.

"So!" said Mr Creakle. "This is the young gentleman whose (8.) **t**☐☐☐**h** are to be filed! Turn around."

Mr Creakle's face was (9.) ☐☐**ery**, and his eyes were small, and deep in his head: he had thick (10.) **ve**☐☐☐ in his forehead, a little nose, and a large chin. He was (11.) **b**☐☐**d** on top of his head: and had some thin wet-looking hair that was just turning grey, brushed across each temple, so that the two sides interlaced on his forehead. But the (12.) **ci**☐☐**um**☐☐**a**☐**ce** about him which impressed me most, was that he had no voice, but spoke in a (13.) ☐**h**☐**s**☐**er.** Talking in that feeble way made his (14.) ☐☐**gr**☐**face** so much more angry, and his thick veins so much (15.) **t**☐☐☐**ker.**

"Come here, sir!" said Mr Creakle, (16.) **be**☐**k**☐☐**ing** to me.

"I have the happiness of knowing your (17.) **s**☐**e**☐**f**☐☐ **her,"** whispered

12. DAVID COPPERFIELD (CONT.)

Mr Creakle, taking me by the ear; "and a worthy man he is, and a man of a strong (18.) ☐☐ar☐☐t☐r," said Mr Creakle, (19.) p☐☐ch☐☐☐ my ear with (20.) f☐☐oci☐☐s playfulness.

I was very much frightened, and felt, all this while, as if my ear were blazing; he pinched it so hard.

Having good spelling skills is essential for partial word tests. Make sure you look up the meaning of words that you do not know and learn them.

13. PETER PAN

By J.M. Barrie

Fill in the missing letters to complete the words in the following passage.

"Tinker Bell," he called softly, after making sure that the children were asleep, "Tink, where are you?" She was in a jug for the moment, and liking it (1.) e☐tr☐☐☐ly; she had never been in a jug before. "Oh, do come out of that jug, and tell me, do you know where they put my shadow?" The (2.) l☐vel☐☐st tinkle as of golden bells (3.) a☐☐we☐ed him. It is the fairy language. You (4.) ☐rd☐n☐ry children can never hear it, but if you were to hear it you would know that you had heard it once before. Tink said that the shadow was in the big box. She meant the chest of drawers, and Peter jumped at the drawers, scattering their contents to the floor with both hands, as kings toss ha'pence to the crowd. In a moment he had (5.) r☐c☐ve☐ed his shadow, and in his delight he forgot that he had shut Tinker Bell up in the drawer. If he thought at all, but I don't believe he ever thought, it was that he and his shadow, when brought near each other, would join like drops of water, and when they did not he was (6.) ap☐a☐☐ed. He tried to stick it on with soap from the bathroom, but that also failed. A shudder passed through Peter, and he sat on the floor and cried. His sobs woke Wendy, and she sat up in bed. She was not alarmed to see a stranger crying on the nursery floor; she was only (7.) ple☐s☐n☐☐y interested. "Boy!" she said (8.) c☐u☐t☐☐u☐ly, "Why are you crying?"

"I was crying because I can't get my shadow to stick on. Besides, I wasn't crying." "It has come off?" "Yes." Then Wendy saw the shadow on the floor, looking so draggled, and she was (9.) fr☐☐☐t☐ull☐ sorry for Peter. "How awful!" she said, but she could not help (10.) s☐i☐ing when she saw that he had been trying to stick it on with soap. How (11.) e☐a☐t☐y like a boy! Fortunately she knew at once what to do. "It must be (12.) s☐wn on," she said, just a little

13. PETER PAN (CONT.)

(13.) p☐tr☐ni☐in☐☐y. "What's sewn?" he asked. "You're dreadfully

(14.) ☐gn☐r☐nt."

"No, I'm not." But she was (15.) ☐xul☐i☐g in his ignorance. "I shall sew it on for you, my little man," she said, though he was tall as herself, and she got out her housewife [sewing bag], and sewed the shadow on to Peter's foot." I

(16.) dar☐sa☐ it will hurt a little," she warned him.

"Oh, I shan't cry," said Peter, who was already of the opinion that he had never cried in his life. And he clenched his teeth and did not cry, and soon his shadow was behaving properly, though still a little (17.) cr☐ase☐.

"Perhaps I should have ironed it," Wendy said thoughtfully, but Peter, boylike, was

(18.) ☐☐di☐f☐re☐t to (19.) ☐pp☐☐r☐n☐es, and he was now jumping about in the wildest glee. Alas, he had already forgotten that he owed his bliss to Wendy. He thought he had attached the shadow himself. "How clever I am!" he crowed (20.) ra☐t☐ro☐sly, "oh, the cleverness of me!"

14. MY FIRST DAY AT SCHOOL

08:00
08 minutes

Fill in the missing letters to complete the words in the following passage.

I remember that my mother made me a (1.) b☐☐ut☐☐ul new pink coat

with a little badge and I (2.) i☐☐gin☐☐ that school would be like a big party.

(3.) ☐☐l☐☐ve me it was not. I began the day full of (4.) opt☐m☐☐m,

but as I approached the classroom I saw a small boy prostrate and

(5.) po☐n☐i☐g his fists on the floor. His sobs had the (6.) ☐ffe☐t

of turning my excitement into fear and trepidation. My mother

(7.) ac☐☐☐pan☐☐d me into the massive classroom which was awash

with a sea of new faces. She tried to coax me into (8.) m☐☐gl☐☐g

with some of the other children, but most of them were, like me, speechless with

either wonder or nervousness.

I was introduced to my teacher, Mrs Swann, whose name was (9.) s☐☐an☐e

and confusing. How could a lady be a bird, and why was she hugging me?

My mother prepared to leave, reassuring me that she would (10.) re☐☐☐n

later but when was later, and where was the toilet located? She gave me a watery

smile and (11.) ☐☐s☐☐pear☐☐. But if this was going to be such a fun

place, why could I see her peering (12.) an☐i☐☐sly through the window with

tears streaming down her face?

The day went from bad to worse. At dinner time you had to help yourself to

(13.) ☐o☐at☐☐s from a large bowl. As I tried to balance mine on the

spoon, it wobbled in my shaking hand and when Johnny Jugears

(14.) j☐g☐l☐d my arm, it went flying across the table into Mary Winger's

lap. She screamed her head off and I can still see her tonsils now. Things began to

(15.) p☐r☐ up a little when the teacher proceeded to read us a story. It was

The Tinder Box where the dog has eyes as big as saucers.

14. MY FIRST DAY AT SCHOOL (CONT.)

She asked us to raise our hands if we had any (16.) ☐u☐s☐i☐ns.
Mine shot in the air lots of times but (17.) un☐☐r☐u☐☐☐ely my finger
shot up Mary's nose and she bawled again. At the end of the day, I was so
(18.) re☐☐☐ve☐ to be re-united with my mother who had promised me all
manner of delights if I had been good. As I left, I waved gaily at the teacher
(19.) in☐a☐dl☐ congratulating myself on surviving the whole school experience.
I remembered my manners and said politely as I had been taught,

"Goodbye, Mrs Swamp. Thank you for the story. It was a (20.) p☐☐asu☐e

to meet you."

"Indeed" she replied through gritted teeth. "See you tomorrow".

Oh my goodness, the shock and horror to my poor five-year-old self.

Why had no one thought to inform me that I had to come back again the next day!

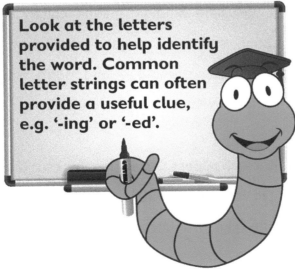

Look at the letters provided to help identify the word. Common letter strings can often provide a useful clue, e.g. '-ing' or '-ed'.

15. WAR HORSE
By Michael Morpurgo

08:00
08 minutes

Fill in the missing letters to complete the words in the following passage.

Albert was about the same (1.) h☐☐☐ht as me and talked so gently as

he (2.) ap☐r☐☐☐ched that I was (3.) i☐med☐☐tely calmed and not a

little (4.) in☐rig☐☐d, and so stood where I was (5.) ag☐☐☐st the

wall. I jumped at first when he (6.) t☐☐☐c☐ed me but could see at once that

he meant me no harm. He (7.) sm☐☐☐hed my back first and then my neck,

talking all the (8.) ☐h☐le about what a fine time we would have together, how

I would grow up to be the (9.) s☐a☐t☐st horse in the whole wide

(10.) w☐☐☐d, and how we would go out hunting together. After a bit he began

to rub me gently with his coat. He rubbed me until I was dry and then dabbed

(11.) sa☐☐ed water onto my face where the skin had been rubbed raw.

He (12.) b☐o☐☐ht in some sweet hay and a bucket of cool, deep water.

I do not (13.) bel☐☐ve he stopped talking all the time. As he turned

to go out of the stable I called out to him to thank him and he seemed to

(14.) ☐nder☐☐ and for he smiled (15.) bro☐d☐y and

(16.) s☐☐☐ked my nose.

"We'll get along, you and I," he said kindly. "I shall call you Joey, only because it

(17.) r☐y☐☐s with Zoey, and then maybe, yes maybe (18.) be☐☐☐s☐

it suits you. I'll be out again in the morning – and don't worry, I'll look after you. I

(19.) ☐☐om☐se you that. Sweet dreams, Joey."

"You should never talk to horses, Albert," said his mother from outside. "They never

understand you. They're stupid creatures. (20.) ☐☐stin☐te and stupid, that's

what your father says, and he's known horses all his life."

SUPER SYNONYMS

Help Billy find the words hidden in the word search. They are all synonyms of the words below! See if you can do this without checking the answers below.

1.) enormous

2.) luminous

3.) ferocious

4.) stout

5.) intrigued

6.) immediately

7.) appalled

8.) ignorant

9.) perk

10.) mingling

Don't forget a synonym is a word that means the same, or almost the same, as another word.

u	a	t	r	b	x	e	s	a	l	y	p
y	n	s	h	o	c	k	e	d	a	l	l
l	v	e	o	s	g	n	a	v	q	t	f
t	i	w	d	t	o	e	d	a	s	n	a
n	o	n	a	u	g	h	s	n	b	a	s
a	v	n	e	s	c	a	r	t	t	t	c
t	a	l	y	r	o	a	o	a	n	s	i
s	k	r	e	f	l	e	t	g	a	n	n
n	b	e	l	h	o	i	u	e	i	i	a
i	n	p	o	u	s	c	n	k	d	g	t
e	g	a	v	a	s	n	d	p	a	e	e
r	s	g	m	e	a	d	z	o	r	s	d
m	t	d	u	t	l	j	r	s	a	h	c
s	c	o	m	b	i	n	i	n	g	e	t

colossal	1	instantly	6
radiant	2	shocked	7
savage	3	uneducated	8
rotund	4	advantage	9
fascinated	5	combining	10

16. THE ADVENTURES OF TOM SAWYER
by Mark Twain

Fill in the missing letters to complete the words in the following passage.

An imaginative and mischievous boy named Tom Sawyer lives with his Aunt Polly and his brother Sid. In this extract, Tom is at school and not best pleased, until his loose tooth takes his attention.

Monday morning found Tom Sawyer miserable. Monday morning (1.) **a**☐☐**ays** found him so — because it began (2.) **anot**☐**e**☐ week's slow suffering in school. He generally began that day with wishing he had had no intervening (3.) **hol**☐**d**☐**y**, it made the going into captivity and fetters again so much more odious.

Tom lay (4.) **thi**☐☐**ing**. Presently it (5.) **oc**☐**ur**☐**ed** to him that he wished he was sick; then he could stay home from (6.) **s**☐**h**☐**ol**. Here was a vague possibility. He canvassed his (7.) **syst**☐☐. No ailment was found, and he investigated again. This time he thought he could detect colicky symptoms, and he (8.) **b**☐**g**☐**n** to encourage them with (9.) **cons**☐**der**☐**ble** hope. But they soon grew feeble, and presently died wholly away. He reflected further. Suddenly he discovered (10.) **s**☐**m**☐**th**☐☐**g**. One of his upper front (11.) **t**☐☐**th** was loose. This was (12.) **l**☐☐**ky**; he was about to begin to groan, as a "starter", as he called it, when it occurred to him that if he came into court with that (13.) **argu**☐**en**☐, his aunt would pull it out, and that would hurt. So he thought he (14.) **w**☐**ul**☐ hold the tooth in reserve for the present, and seek further. Nothing offered for some little time, and then he (15.) **re**☐**em**☐**ere**☐ hearing the doctor tell about a (16.) **cert**☐☐**n** thing that laid up a patient for two or three weeks and threatened to make him lose a (17.) **fin**☐**e**☐. So the boy (18.) **eag**☐**r**☐**y** drew his sore toe from under the sheet and held it up for inspection. But now he did not know the

16. THE ADVENTURES OF TOM SAWYER (CONT.)

necessary symptoms. (19.) **Ho**⬚**eve**⬚ , it seemed well worthwhile to chance it, so he fell to (20.) **gr**⬚⬚**ning** with considerable spirit.

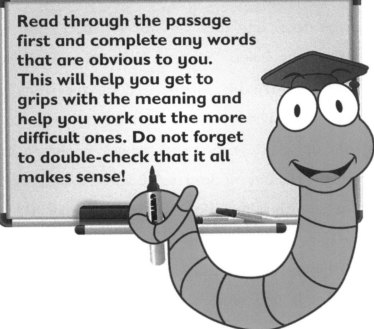

Read through the passage first and complete any words that are obvious to you. This will help you get to grips with the meaning and help you work out the more difficult ones. Do not forget to double-check that it all makes sense!

17. THE JUNGLE BOOK
By Rudyard Kipling

Fill in the missing letters to complete the words in the following passage.

Mowgli is a little Indian boy who has been raised in the jungle by wolves. In this extract, his friends Bagheera (a panther) and Baloo (a bear) are trying to rescue him from some vain and foolish monkeys.

The next thing he remembered was (1.) **f☐☐ling** hands on his legs and arms — hard, (2.) **st☐o☐g**, little hands — and then a swash of (3.) **br☐☐ches** in his face, and then he was (4.) **st☐ri☐g** down through the swaying boughs as Baloo (5.) **w☐k☐** the jungle with his deep (6.) **cr☐☐s** and Bagheera (7.) **bo☐nd☐d** up the trunk with every (8.) **t☐☐t☐** bared. The Bandar-log howled with (9.) **trium☐☐** and scuffled away to the (10.) **up☐☐r** branches where Bagheera dared not (11.) **f☐lo☐**, shouting: "He has noticed us! Bagheera has noticed us. All the Jungle-People (12.) **a☐mir☐** us for our skill and our (13.) **c☐☐ning.**" Then they began their flight; and the flight of the Monkey-People through tree-land is one of the things (14.) **no☐o☐y** can (15.) **de☐☐☐ibe**. They have their regular roads and crossroads, up hills and down hills, all (16.) **la☐d** out from fifty to seventy or a hundred feet above ground, and by these they can travel even at night if (17.) **nec☐☐☐ary**. Two of the strongest monkeys caught Mowgli under the arms and (18.) **sw☐☐g** off with him through the treetops, twenty feet at a bound. Had they been alone they could have gone twice as fast, but the boy's (19.) **w☐i☐ht** held them back. Sick and giddy as Mowgli was, he could not help enjoying the wild rush, though the (20.) **gl☐mp☐es** of earth far down below frightened him, and

17. THE JUNGLE BOOK (CONT.)

the terrible check and jerk at the end of the swing over nothing but empty air brought his heart between his teeth.

In Partial Word passages, spelling is key! Make sure you are familiar with well-known tricky words such as describe, necessary and glimpses, so that you get vowels, double letters and unusual digraphs in the right places.

18. THE FROG PRINCE
By the Brothers Grimm

07:00
07 minutes

Fill in the missing letters to complete the words in the following passage.

This extract begins the story of a princess who meets a frog who is later revealed to be her handsome prince but who is currently under the spell of a wicked witch.

In the old times, when it was still of some use to wish for the thing one (1.) w☐☐t☐d, there lived a king whose daughters were all handsome, but the (2.) y☐☐ng☐st was so (3.) b☐☐☐ti☐☐l that the sun himself, who has seen so much, wondered each time he (4.) ☐ho☐e over her because of her beauty. Near the royal (5.) c☐☐t☐e there was a great, dark wood, and in the wood (6.) ☐n☐☐r an old linden-tree was a well; and (7.) ☐he☐ the day was hot, the king's (8.) d☐☐ght☐r used to go forth into the wood and sit by the brink of the cool well, and if the time (9.) s☐☐m☐d long, she would take out a golden ball, and (10.) t☐☐o☐ it up and catch it again, and this was her (11.) fa☐☐☐rit☐ pastime. Now it (12.) h☐☐☐☐n☐d one day that the golden ball, (13.) in☐☐☐ad of falling back into the Maiden's little hand (14.) w☐☐☐h had sent it aloft, dropped to the (15.) g☐☐u☐d near the (16.) e☐☐e of the well and rolled in. The king's daughter followed it with her (17.) e☐☐s as it sank, but the well was deep, so deep that the bottom (18.) ☐o☐☐d not be seen. Then she began to weep, and she wept and wept as if she could never be (19.) c☐☐fo☐☐ed. And in the midst of her weeping she heard a (20.) v☐☐c☐ saying to her, "What ails thee, King's daughter? Thy tears would melt a heart of stone." And when she looked to see

18. THE FROG PRINCE (CONT.)

where the voice came from, there was nothing but a frog stretching his thick, ugly head out of the water.

If you are stuck, look for clues that might suggest familiar letter combinations such as th, sh and wh. They pop up everywhere and will definitely help you!

19. REBECCA OF SUNNYBROOK FARM
By Kate Douglas Wiggin

07:00
07 minutes

Fill in the missing letters to complete the words in the following passage.

Rebecca lives with her two aunts who are kind but stern. In this extract, she would very much like to put on the new dress that one aunt has made for her. However, there is no one at home to give her permission to wear it.

Rebecca found the side (1.) **do**☐**r** locked, but she knew that the key was under the step, and so of course did everybody else in Riverboro, for they all did about the same thing with it. She (2.) **u**☐☐**ocked** the door and went into the dining-room to find her lunch laid on the table and a note from Aunt Jane saying that they had gone to Moderation with Mrs. Robinson in her carryall. Rebecca swallowed a (3.) **p**☐☐**ce** of bread and butter, and flew up the front (4.) **sta**☐☐**s** to her bedroom. On the bed lay the pink gingham dress finished by Aunt Jane's kind hands. Could she, dare she, wear it without asking? Did the occasion justify a new costume, or (5.) **wo**☐☐**d** her aunts think she ought to keep it for the concert?

"I'll (6.) **w**☐☐**r** it," thought Rebecca. "They're not here to ask, and maybe they wouldn't mind a bit; it's only gingham (7.) **a**☐☐**er** all, and wouldn't be so grand if it wasn't new, and hadn't tape trimming on it, and wasn't (8.) **p**☐☐**k**."

She unbraided her (9.) **t**☐**o** pig-tails, combed out the waves of her hair and (10.) **ti**☐☐**them** back with a ribbon, changed her shoes, and then (11.) **sli**☐☐**ed** on the pretty frock, managing to (12.) **fas**☐☐**n** all but the three middle buttons, which she reserved for Emma Jane.

Then her eye fell on her cherished pink sunshade, the exact match, and the (13.) **gi**☐☐**s** had never seen it. It wasn't quite appropriate for (14.) **s**☐☐**ool**,

19. REBECCA OF SUNNYBROOK FARM (CONT.)

but she needn't take it into the room; she would (15.) **wr**☐☐it in a piece of paper, just show it, and carry it (16.) **co**☐☐**ng** home. She glanced in the parlour looking-glass (17.) **downst**☐☐**rs** and was electrified at the vision. It seemed almost as if beauty of apparel could go no further than that heavenly pink gingham dress! The sparkle of her eyes, glow of her (18.) **ch**☐☐**ks**, sheen of her falling (19.) **ha**☐☐, passed unnoticed in the all-conquering charm of the rose-coloured garment. Goodness! It was twenty (20.) **min**☐☐**es** to one and she would be late.

Sometimes you will think that there are two possibilities for a word, e.g. p_ _k and ch_ _ks. Think about the sense of the two possibilities. Would Rebecca's dress be PINK or PUNK? When describing her face, would the word be CHEEKS or CHICKS? Jot the possibilities down and you will soon find the right answer!

20. THE VELVETEEN RABBIT
By Margery Williams

07:00
07 minutes

Fill in the missing letters to complete the words in the following passage.

The Velveteen Rabbit was a Christmas present for a boy who has now almost forgotten about him. He lives in the nursery cupboard amongst a lot of other toys.

For a long *time* he lived in the toy (1.) **cu**☐☐**oard** or on the nursery floor, and no one (2.) **thou**☐☐**t** very much (3.) **ab**☐☐**t** him. He was naturally shy and, being only made of velveteen, some of the more expensive toys quite snubbed him. The mechanical toys were very superior, and looked down upon everyone else; they were full of modern (4.) **ide**☐☐, and pretended they were real. The model boat, who had (5.) **li**☐**ed** through two seasons end lost most of his paint, caught the tone from them and never missed an opportunity of referring to his rigging in technical terms. The Rabbit could not claim to be a model of (6.) **any**☐☐**ing**, for he didn't know that real rabbits (7.) **exis**☐☐**d**; he thought they were all stuffed with sawdust like himself, and he (8.) **unders**☐☐☐**d** that sawdust was quite out-of-date and should never be mentioned in modern circles. Even Timothy, the jointed (9.) **woo**☐☐**n** lion, who was made by the disabled soldiers, and should have had broader views, put on airs and (10.) **prete**☐☐**ed** he was connected with Government. Between them all the (11.) **p**☐☐**r** little Rabbit was made to feel himself very (12.) **insignifi**☐☐☐**t** and commonplace, and the only person who was kind to him at all was the Skin Horse.

The Skin Horse had lived longer in the nursery than any of the others. He was so old that his brown coat was bald in (13.) **p**☐**t**☐**hes** and showed the seams (14.) **under**☐☐☐**th**, and most of the hairs in his (15.) **ta**☐☐ had been pulled out to string (16.) **b**☐☐**d** necklaces. He was wise, for he had seen a long succession of mechanical toys arrive to boast and swagger, and by-and-by break

20. THE VELVETEEN RABBIT (CONT.)

(17.) **the** ☐ ☐ mainsprings and pass away, and he knew that they were only toys, and (18.) **w** ☐ ☐ ☐ **d** never turn into anything else. For nursery (19.) **mag** ☐ ☐ is very strange and (20.) **wonder** ☐ ☐ ☐ , and only those playthings that are old and wise and experienced like the Skin Horse understand all about it.

Many of the passages you come across will be from classic children's literature, which means they were published a long time ago and therefore the language might sound quite formal and old-fashioned, and there might be references to unfamiliar things from the past. Reading classic literature will build both your vocabulary and your understanding of more complex sentence structures and use of punctuation.

STRENUOUS SPELLINGS

In Cloze passages, you need a strong grasp of spelling patterns.

There are plenty of ways of learning the more challenging words. For example, to help you remember the tricky word *necessary,* think of '1 collar but 2 socks' or 'one coffee, two sugars' for the 'c' and 'ss' issue, which often catches children out (and some adults!).

Another useful technique is creating catchy mnemonics. Mnemonics can be rhymes or silly sentences that stick in your mind – often the sillier they are, the better they are for remembering.

For instance, to help with the spelling of *rhythm,* the following mnemonic can be useful:

Rhythm **H**as **Y**our **T**wo **H**ips **M**oving

One memorable mnemonic for *because* is:

Big **E**lephants **C**an **A**lways **U**nderstand **S**mall **E**lephants

Have a go at creating your own mnemonics in the table below.

laugh	beautiful	geography
l	b	g
a	e	e
u	a	o
g	u	g
h	t	r
	i	a
	f	p
	u	h
	l	y

When you have finished, compare your mnemonic with someone else's. Which is the easiest to remember?

SECTION 3:
WORD BANKS

21. THE RAILWAY CHILDREN
By Edith Nesbit

extremely	engineer	besides	there	aloud
eldest	excellent	suppose	occasions	coloured
youngest	their	interestingly	ordinary	merry
favourites	refurnishing	unjust	convenience	tiled

Write the correct word from the bank above to fill the space. (Don't forget to capitalise the initial letter if the word is at the start of a sentence).

They were not railway children to begin with. I don't (1.) _____ they had

ever thought about railways except as a means of getting to Maskelyne and Cook's,

the Pantomime, Zoological Gardens and Madame Tussaud's. They were first

(2.) _____ suburban children and they lived with (3.) _____

father in an ordinary red-bricked fronted villa with (4.) _____ glass in the

front door, a (5.) _____ passage that was called a hall, a bathroom with

hot and cold water, electric bells, French Windows and a good deal of white paint, and

"every modern (6.) _____," as the house-agents say.

There were three of them. Roberta was the (7.) _____. Of course, mothers

never have (8.) _____ but if their mother had had a favourite, it might

have been Roberta. Next came Peter who wished to be an (9.) _____

when he grew up and the (10.) _____ was Phyllis, who meant

(11.) _____ well.

Mother did not spend all her time in paying dull calls to dull ladies, and sitting dully

at home waiting for dull ladies to pay calls to her. She was almost always

(12.) _____, ready to play with the children, and read to them, and help

them to do their home-lessons. (13.) _____ this she used to write stories

for them while they were at school and read them (14.) _____ after tea,

and she always made up funny pieces of poetry for their birthdays and for other great

21. THE RAILWAY CHILDREN (CONT.)

(15.) _____, such as christenings of the new kittens,

(16.) _____ of the doll's house, or the time when they were getting over the

mumps.

These three lucky children always had everything they needed: pretty clothes, good

fires, a lovely nursery with heaps of toys, and a Mother Goose wallpaper. They had a

kind and (17.) _____ nursemaid and a dog who was called James, and who

was their very own. They also had a father who was just perfect – never cross, never

(18.) _____, and always ready for a game – at least, if at any time he was

not ready, he always had an (19.) _____ reason for it, and explained the

reason to the children so (20.) _____ and funnily that they felt sure he

couldn't help himself.

Fill in the answers that you are confident about. The process of elimination will then help you to answer the other questions.

22. THE WONDERFUL CITY OF OZ

06:00
06 minutes

tint	lemonade	carried	building	panes
pushed	protected	uniform	glittering	offered
lined	dressed	studded	spoke	dazzled
greenish	contented	answered	clothes	prosperous

Write the correct word from the bank above to fill the space.

Even with eyes (1.) _____ by the green spectacles, Dorothy and her friends

were at first (2.) _____ by the brilliancy of the wonderful city. The

streets were (3.) _____ with beautiful houses all built of green marble

and (4.) _____ everywhere with sparkling emeralds. They walked over

a pavement of the same green marble, and where the blocks were joined together

rows of emeralds, set closely, and (5.) _____ in the brightness of

the sun. The window (6.) _____ were green glass; even the sky

above the City had a green (7.) _____, and the rays of the sun were

green. There were many people – men, women and children – walking about, and

these were all (8.) _____ in green clothes and had (9.) _____

skins. They looked at Dorothy and her strangely assorted company with wondering

eyes, and the children all ran away and hid behind their mothers when they saw

the Lion; but no one (10.) _____ to them. Many shops stood in the

street, and Dorothy saw that everything in them was green. Green Candy and green

popcorn were (11.) _____ for sale, as well as green shoes, green hats and

green (12.) _____ of all sorts. At one place a man was selling green

(13.) _____, and when the children bought it Dorothy could see that they

paid for it with green pennies. There seemed to be no horses nor animals of any kind;

the men (14.) _____ things around in little green carts, which

they (15.) _____ before them. Everyone seemed happy and

(16.) _____ and (17.) _____. The Guardian of the Gates led

them through the streets until they came to a big (18.) _____,

22. THE WONDERFUL CITY OF OZ (CONT.)

exactly in the middle of the City, which was the Palace of Oz the Great Wizard. There

was a soldier before the door, dressed in a green (19.) _____ and

wearing a long green beard. "Here are strangers," said the Guardian of the Gates to

him, "and they demand to see the Great Oz." "Step inside," (20.) _____

the soldier, "and I will carry your message to him."

Reading beyond the gap can help you put the sentence into context.

Also, make sure you spell the words correctly when copying them from the word bank.

23. DEEP SEA WILDLIFE

06:00
06 minutes

blackness	grabbing	survive	adapted	sieve
relatives	teeth	patrol	searching	similar
particles	sunlight	fishing	enormous	largest
stomachs	hundreds	extraordinary	surface	themselves

Write the correct word from the bank above to fill the space. (Don't forget to capitalise the initial letter if the word is at the start of a sentence).

At the bottom of the sea lies the (1.) _____ wildlife habitat on Earth. No

plants can grow because there is no (2.) _____ However, in the vast

(3.) _____ many (4.) _____ creatures live. These animals are

found nowhere else on earth. They have (5.) _____ to

(6.) _____ in water pressure that is up to 1,000 times greater than

at the (7.) _____ Some other fish have (8.) _____ mouths and

long curved-back (9.) _____ for (10.) _____ and swallowing

prey. These fish have huge (11.) _____ which stretch to hold animals that

are even bigger than (12.) _____. Many animals on the deep-sea

floor, like shrimps, krill, worms, brittlestars and shellfish (13.) _____

the mud (14.) _____ for tiny (15.) _____ of food.

(16.) _____ of deep-sea fish glow in the dark, including anglerfish, lantern

fish and slickhead. Dozens of different anglerfish (17.) _____ the ocean

depths. They are (18.) _____ to their (19.) _____, the shallow-water

angelfish, in the way they fish for food. They use a long flexible spine on their

back as a (20.) _____ rod.

24. AUSTRALIA

hemisphere	vivid	formerly	magnificent	shallow
expanse	spans	varied	shoals	marine
colony	renowned	inhabitants	vast	interior
world's	dart	city's	impressive	located

Write the correct word from the bank above to fill the space. (Don't forget to capitalise the initial letter if the word is at the start of a sentence).

Known to the British as "The Land Down Under", Australia is the sixth largest country

in the world. (1.) _____ in the southern (2.) _____ between

the Indian and Pacific oceans, it boasts many (3.) _____ landscapes

including tropical rainforests, snow-capped mountains and a (4.) _____

desert throughout its (5.) _____ known as The Outback.

It is in the centre of this (6.) _____ that a giant mass of sandstone lies Uluru,

(7.) _____ known as Ayers Rock. An (8.) _____ 335 metres high,

it is a world- (9.) _____ sight of natural beauty, especially at sunset when it appears

to change colour.

Just below the (10.) _____ seas off the north east coast of Australia lies

the Great Barrier Reef. This is one of the (11.) _____ most precious

(12.) _____ environments, a truly (13.) _____ ecosystem.

Here, (14.) _____ of brightly coloured fish (15.) _____ amongst delicate

fingers of (16.) _____ coral, and dolphins play in the waves.

Sydney is the largest city in Australia. Founded in 1788 as a prison

(17.) _____, it now has more than four million (18.) _____.

The (19.) _____ most famous landmarks include its Opera House and the grand

Sydney Harbour Bridge which (20.) _____ the natural bay of Port Jackson.

25. WHITE FANG

By Jack London

06:00
06 minutes

cartridges	darkness	wolves	baby	announced
many's	ought	lunging	sure	decoy
wolf's	attention	intruder	had	cogitated
observing	of	animal's	strained	spluttering

Write the correct word from the bank above to fill the space.

A sound among the dogs attracted the men's (1.) _____. One Ear was uttering quick, eager whines, (2.) _____ at the length of his stick toward the darkness, and desisting now and again in order to make frantic attacks on the stick with his teeth.

"Look at that, Bill," Henry whispered.

Full into the firelight, with a stealthy, sidelong movement, glided a doglike animal. It moved with commingled mistrust and daring, cautiously (3.) _____ the men, its attention fixed on the dogs. One Ear (4.) _____ the full length of the stick toward the (5.) _____ and whined with eagerness.

"That fool One Ear don't seem scairt much," Bill said in a low tone.

"It's a she-wolf," Henry whispered back, "an' that accounts for Fatty an' Frog. She's the (6.) _____ for the pack. She draws out the dog an' then all the rest pitches in an' eats 'm up."

The fire crackled. A log fell apart with a loud (7.) _____ noise. At the sound (8.) _____ it the strange animal leaped back into the (9.) _____. "Henry, I'm a-thinkin'," Bill (10.) _____. "Thinkin' what?"

25. WHITE FANG (CONT.)

"I'm a-thinkin' that was the one I lambasted with the club."

"Ain't the slightest doubt in the world," was Henry's response.

"An' right here I want to remark," Bill went on, "that (11.) _____ familiarity

with campfires is suspicious an' immoral."

"It knows for certain more'n a self-respectin' wolf (12.) _____ to know,"

Henry agreed. "A wolf that knows enough to come in with the dogs at feedin' time

has (13.) _____ experiences."

"Ol' Villan had a dog once that run away with the wolves", Bill (14.) _____, aloud.

"I ought to know. I shot it out of the pack in a moose pasture over 'on Little Stick.

An' Ol' Villan cried like a (15.) _____. Hadn't seen it for three years, he said.

Been with the (16.) _____ all that time."

"I reckon you've called the turn, Bill. That (17.) _____ a dog, an' it's eaten

fish (18.) _____ the time from the hand of man."

"An' if I get a chance at it, that wolf that's a dog'll be jes' meat," Bill declared. "We

can't afford to lose no more animals."

"But you've only got three (19.) _____," Henry objected.

"I'll wait for a dead (20.) _____ shot," was the reply.

AWESOME ANTONYMS

Help Billy complete this antonyms crossword. There are some letters already in the crossword to help you. Good luck!

Down

1. contented
2. vivid
5. interior
9. merry

Across

3. vast
4. healthy
6. shallow
7. faithful
8. similar
10. pretentious
11. uniform
12. protected

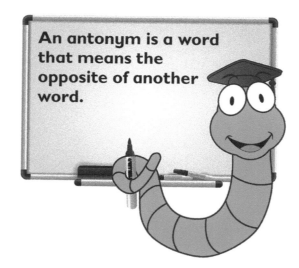

An antonym is a word that means the opposite of another word.

Teachitright Teaser: Look through this Cloze workbook and see if you can find 10 more antonyms.

**THIS PAGE HAS DELIBERATELY
BEEN LEFT BLANK**

26. THE SELFISH GIANT
By Oscar Wilde

stop	beautiful	friend	order	ogre
there	nobody	over	determined	wall
conversation	cried	sweetly	here	gruff
used	afternoon	broke	soft	bore

Write the correct word from the bank above to fill the space.

In this extract we are introduced to the selfish Giant and his beautiful garden, which he is reluctant to share.

Every (1.) _____, as they were coming from school, the children

(2.) _____ to go and play in the Giant's garden.

It was a large lovely garden, with (3.) _____ green grass. Here and

(4.) _____ over the grass stood (5.) _____ flowers

like stars, and there were twelve peach-trees that in the spring-time

(6.) _____ out into delicate blossoms of pink and pearl, and in the autumn

(7.) _____ rich fruit. The birds sat on the trees and sang so

(8.) _____ that the children used to (9.) _____ their

games in (10.) _____ to listen to them. "How happy we are

(11.) _____!" they (12.) _____ to each other.

One day the Giant came back. He had been to visit his (13.) _____ the

Cornish (14.) _____, and had stayed with him for seven years. After the

seven years were (15.) _____ he had said all that he had to say, for his

(16.) _____ was limited, and he (17.) _____ to return

to his own castle. When he arrived he saw the children playing in the garden.

26. THE SELFISH GIANT (CONT.)

"What are you doing here?" he cried in a very (18.) _____ voice, and the children ran away.

"My own garden is my own garden," said the Giant; "Everyone can understand that, and I will allow (19.) _____ to play in it but myself." So he built a high (20.) _____ all round it, and put up a notice-board.

> **TRESPASSERS**
> **WILL BE**
> **PROSECUTED**

He was a very selfish Giant.

Don't rush straight into Word Bank passages. Take time to read through the word bank and note any homophones or similar words, and tricky ones where you are not sure of the meaning. This will give you an idea of what the passage is about and help you drop the easy words into the gaps when you do begin.

27. HEIDI

By Johanna Spyri

fulfilled	flew	sleep	mightily	wealth
perfume	steps	exquisite	life	again
well	reached	brim	grasp	firm
joyously	glad	goats	wherever	dry

Write the correct word from the bank above to fill the space.

Heidi is living in the Alps with her grandfather. Her friend Clara, who is paralysed, is visiting her there. When Heidi's friend, Peter, destroys Clara's wheelchair in a fit of jealousy, Clara is forced to try to walk.

Heidi rapturously exclaimed: "Oh, Clara, can you really? Can you walk? Oh, can you take

(1.) _____ now? Oh, if only grandfather would come! Now you can

walk, Clara, now you can walk," she kept on saying (2.) _____.

Clara held on tight to the children, but with every new step she became more

(3.) _____.

"Now you can come up here every day," cried Heidi. "Now we can walk

(4.) _____ we want to and you don't have to be pushed in a chair any

more. Now you'll be able to walk all your (5.) _____. Oh, what joy!"

Clara's greatest wish, to be able to be (6.) _____ like other people,

had been (7.) _____ at last. It was not very far to the flowering field.

Soon they (8.) _____ it and sat down among the

(9.) _____ of bloom. It was the first time that Clara had ever rested

on the (10.) _____ warm earth. All about them the flowers nodded and

exhaled their (11.) _____. It was a scene of

(12.) _____ beauty.

27. HEIDI (CONT.)

The two children could hardly (13.) _____ this happiness that had come

to them. It filled their hearts to the (14.) _____ and made them silent.

Peter also lay motionless, for he had gone to (15.) _____.

Thus the hours (16.) _____ and the day was long past noon. Suddenly all

the (17.) _____ arrived, for they had been seeking the children. They did

not like to graze in the flowers, and were (18.) _____ when Peter awoke

with their loud bleating. The poor boy was (19.) _____ bewildered, for he

had dreamt that the rolling-chair with the red cushions stood (20.) _____

before his eyes.

Use your knowledge of word groups to help you choose correctly. Sometimes it will clearly be a noun or a verb which is missing and you can eliminate any other word type.

28. ROBIN HOOD
Adapted from 'The Book of Romance' by HJ Ford

arrow	unbuckled	spanned	falls	anger
walking	arms	into	one	midst
river	stranger	blew	tumbled	would
horn	waded	their	name	hand

Write the correct word from the bank above to fill the space.

This extract tells the story of how Robin first met his greatest friend, Little John.

One day Robin was (1.) _____ alone in the wood, and reached a river

(2.) _____ by a very narrow bridge, over which

(3.) _____ man only could pass. In the (4.) _____

stood a stranger, and Robin bade him go back and let him go over. "I am no man of yours,"

was all the answer Robin got, and in (5.) _____ he drew his bow and

fitted an (6.) _____ to it. "Would you shoot a man who has no

(7.) _____ but a staff?" asked the stranger in scorn; and with shame

Robin laid down his bow, and (8.) _____ an oaken stick at his side.

"We will fight till one of us (9.) _____ into the water," he said;

and fight they did, till the stranger planted a blow so well that Robin rolled over

(10.) _____ the river. "You are a brave soul," said he, when he had

(11.) _____ to land, and he (12.) _____ a blast

with his (13.) _____ which brought fifty good fellows, clad in green, to

the little bridge. "Have you fallen into the (14.) _____ that your clothes

are wet?" asked one; and Robin made answer. "No, but this (15.) _____,

fighting on the bridge, got the better of me, and (16.) _____ me into the

stream."

At this the foresters seized the stranger, and (17.) _____ have ducked him

had not (18.) _____ leader bade them stop, and begged the stranger to

28. ROBIN HOOD (CONT.)

stay with them and make one of themselves. "Here is my (19.) _____,"
replied the stranger, "and my heart with it. My (20.) _____, if you would
know it, is John Little."

Some words seem to fit into more than one space but remember you can only use each word once. Read through the text when you have finished to check!

29. THE SECRET GARDEN
by Frances Hodgson Burnett

hopped	hand	human	together	flew
key	buried	knowing	hole	flowers
waistcoat	forgot	breast	whisper	pretty
earth	worm	something	frightened	brass

Write the correct word from the bank above to fill the space.

Mary Lennox has gone to live at her uncle's house in Yorkshire. In this extract, she is searching for a way into the mysterious garden that has remained a secret for ten years.

He chirped, and talked, and coaxed and he (1.) _____, and flirted his

tail and twittered. It was as if he were talking. His red (2.) _____ was

like satin and he puffed his tiny (3.) _____ out and was so fine and so

grand and so (4.) _____ that it was really as if he were showing her

how important and like a (5.) _____ person a robin could be. Mistress

Mary (6.) _____ that she had ever been contrary in her life when he

allowed her to draw closer and closer to him, and bend down and talk and try to make

(7.) _____ like robin sounds.

The flower-bed was not quite bare. It was bare of (8.) _____ because the

perennial plants had been cut down for their winter rest, but there were tall shrubs

and low ones which grew (9.) _____ at the back of the bed, and as the

robin hopped about under them she saw him hop over a small pile of freshly turned

up (10.) _____. He stopped on it to look for a

(11.) _____. The earth had been turned up because a dog had been

trying to dig up a mole and he had scratched quite a deep (12.) _____.

29. THE SECRET GARDEN (CONT.)

Mary looked at it, not really (13.) _____ why the hole was there, and as

she looked she saw something almost (14.) _____ in the newly-turned

soil. It was something like a ring of rusty iron or (15.) _____ and

when the robin (16.) _____ up into a tree nearby she put out her

(17.) _____ and picked the ring up. It was more than a ring, however; it

was an old (18.) _____ which looked as if it had been buried a long time.

Mistress Mary stood up and looked at it with an almost (19.) _____ face

as it hung from her finger.

"Perhaps it has been buried for ten years," she said in a (20.) _____.

"Perhaps it is the key to the garden!"

Don't forget that if the missing word is preceded by 'a', it must begin with a consonant. If 'an' comes before it, the word will begin with a vowel.

30. THE ELEPHANT'S CHILD
by Rudyard Kipling

seen	wood	crocodile	throwing	could
spanked	helped	politely	winked	tail
close	including	person	little	bank
tears	whisper	hairy	more	useful

Write the correct word from the bank above to fill the space.

The Elephant's Child is on a journey through Africa to find the answer to an important question: "What does the Crocodile have for dinner?"

He said good-bye very politely to the Bi-Coloured-Python-Rock-Snake, and

(1.) _____ to coil him up on the rock again, and went on, a little warm,

but not at all astonished, eating melons, and (2.) _____ the rind about,

because he (3.) _____ not pick it up, till he trod on what he thought was

a log of (4.) _____ at the very edge of the great grey-green, greasy

Limpopo River, all set about with fever-trees.

But it was really the Crocodile, O Best Beloved, and the Crocodile

(5.) _____ one eye — like this!

"'Scuse me," said the Elephant's Child most politely, "but do you happen to have

(6.) _____ a (7.) _____ in these promiscuous parts?"

Then the Crocodile winked the other eye, and lifted half his (8.) _____

out of the mud; and the Elephant's Child stepped back most politely, because he did not

wish to be spanked again.

"Come hither, Little One," said the Crocodile. "Why do you ask such things?"

30. THE ELEPHANT'S CHILD (CONT.)

"'Scuse me," said the Elephant's Child most (9.) _____, "but my father

has (10.) _____ me, my mother has spanked me, not to mention my tall

aunt, the Ostrich, and my tall uncle, the Giraffe, who can kick ever so hard, as well as

my broad aunt, the Hippopotamus, and my (11.) _____ uncle, the Baboon,

and (12.) _____ the Bi-Coloured-Python-Rock-Snake, with the scalesome,

flailsome tail, just up the bank, who spanks harder than any of them; and so, if it's

quite all the same to you, I don't want to be spanked any (13.) _____."

"Come hither, Little One," said the Crocodile, "for I am the Crocodile," and he wept

crocodile (14.) _____ to show it was quite true.

Then the Elephant's Child grew all breathless, and panted, and kneeled down on the

(15.) _____ and said, "You are the very (16.) _____

I have been looking for all these long days. Will you please tell me what you have for dinner?"

"Come hither, Little One," said the Crocodile, "and I'll (17.) _____."

Then the Elephant's Child put his head down (18.) _____ to

the Crocodile's musky, tusky mouth, and

the Crocodile caught him by his

(19.) _____ nose, which up

to that very week, day, hour, and minute, had

been no bigger than a boot, though much

more (20.) _____.

"I think," said the Crocodile — and he said it

between his teeth, like this — "I think today

I will begin with Elephant's Child!"

If you have enjoyed reading any of these passages, look them up and read more. This passage is from the famous *Just So Stories* by Rudyard Kipling.

AWESOME ADJECTIVES

In Cloze tests, it is useful to know the word group of the word to be placed in the gap: is it an adjective, noun, verb or adverb?

Adjectives modify nouns by giving more information about them. Remember, a noun is a naming word for a person, place or thing. An adjective can appear directly before or after a noun.

Below is a bank of adjectives that need to be placed in the gaps. It's worth considering the context of the sentence to help you place the adjective in the right place. (Each word can only be used once.)

negative	angry	ancient	dreary	energetic
flimsy	hilarious	idle	leafy	mysterious

1. Louise gave us a _____ account of her first days as a teacher.

2. Sandeep was just making _____ conversation.

3. We heard a _____ noise coming from the attic.

4. The weather from the window looked wet and _____.

5. Sally was a _____ person and loved to complain.

6. An _____ crowd approached the Parliament buildings to voice their concerns.

7. John and his family live in a _____ suburb, on the outskirts of London.

8. The _____ Egyptians often relaxed by playing board games.

9. Vicki has an _____ personality.

10. If the fabric is _____ and thin, the jumper is poor quality.

Check at the back of the book to see if you placed the words in the correct sentence.

SECTION 4:
MIXED CLOZE PASSAGES

31. A CHRISTMAS CAROL
By Charles Dickens

Mark the box with a pencil line next to the correct word to complete the sentence.

When Scrooge awoke, it was so dark, that looking out of bed, he could scarcely

(1.)
☐ a. distinguish
☐ b. distribute   the transparent window from the
☐ c. describe

(2.)
☐ a. striking
☐ b. translucent   walls
☐ c. opaque

of his chamber. He was endeavouring to (3.)
☐ a. pierce
☐ b. prise   the darkness with his
☐ c. pursue

ferret eyes, when the chimes of a neighbouring church struck the four quarters. So he

(4.)
☐ a. shouted
☐ b. listened   for the hour. To his great (5.)
☐ c. discussed

☐ a. amusement
☐ b. astounded   the heavy bell
☐ c. astonishment

went on from six to seven, and from seven to eight, and regularly up to twelve; then

stopped. Twelve! It was (6.)
☐ a. past
☐ b. passed   two when he went to bed. The clock was
☐ c. from

wrong. An icicle must have got into the works. Twelve! He touched the spring of his

repeater, to correct this most (7.)
☐ a. prosperous
☐ b. preposterous   clock. Its rapid little pulse
☐ c. preposition

(8.)
☐ a. beet
☐ b. bait   twelve; and stopped. "Why, it isn't possible," said Scrooge, "that I can
☐ c. beat

have (9.)
☐ a. sleeps
☐ b. sleep   through a whole day and far into another night. It isn't possible
☐ c. slept

that anything has happened to the sun, and this twelve at noon! The idea being an

31. A CHRISTMAS CAROL (CONT.)

a. scrambled

alarming one, he (10.) [   ] b. scrabbled   out of bed, and groped his way to the window.

c. scrawled

a. obscured

He was (11.) [   ] b. obliged   to rub the frost off with the sleeve of his dressing-gown

c. obsessed

before he could see anything; and could see very little then. All he could make out

a. raining

was that it was still very (12.) [   ] b. clean   and extremely cold, and that there was no

c. foggy

noise of people running to and fro, and making a great stir, as there

a. unquestionably

(13.) [   ] b. probable   would have been if night had beaten off bright day and

c. questionable

a. possession   a. nervousness

taken (14.) [   ] b. processes of this world. This was a great (15.) [   ] b. relief

c. procession   c. excitement

because "three days after sight of this First of Exchange pay to Mr Ebenezer Scrooge or

a. help

his order", and so forth, would have become a mere United States' (16.) [   ] b. security

c. country

if there were no days to count by.

Scrooge went to bed again, and thought, and thought, and thought it over and

a. perplexed

over, and could make nothing of it. The more he thought, the more (17.) [   ] b. gracious

c. flourished

a. encouraged

he was: and the more he (18.) [   ] b. motivated   not to think, the more

c. endeavoured

(continued over)

31. A CHRISTMAS CAROL (CONT.)

he thought. Marley's Ghost bothered him (19.) ☐ a. extraordinary.
☐ b. exceedingly. Every time he
☐ c. respectively.

resolved within himself, after mature (20.) ☐ a. inquiry
☐ b. belief   that it was all a dream,
☐ c. effort

his mind flew back again, like a strong spring released, to its first position, and

presented the same problem to be worked all through, "Was it a dream or not?"

If you have time, re-read the passage to check your answers.

32. THE WIND IN THE WILLOWS
by Kenneth Grahame

Fill in the missing letters to complete the words in the following passage.

Mole thought his happiness was (1.) c☐mp☐e☐☐ as he meandered

(2.) a☐mles☐☐y along. Suddenly he stood by the edge of a full-fed river.

Never in his life had he seen a river before – this sleek, (3.) s☐nu☐☐s

full-bodied animal, chasing and chuckling, gripping things with a gurgle and leaving

them with a (4.) l☐☐gh, to fling itself on fresh playmates that (5.) s☐oo☐

themselves free, and were caught and held again. All was a-shake and

a-(6.) ☐hiv☐☐, glints and gleams and sparkles, rustle and swirl, chatter and

bubble. The Mole was, (7.) b☐w☐tch☐☐, entranced, fascinated. By the

side of the river he (8.) tr☐t☐☐d as one moves when very small, by the

side of a man who (9.) h☐l☐s one spellbound by exciting stories; and when

(10.) ☐x☐au☐t☐d at last, he sat on the bank, while the river still

(11.) c☐att☐☐ed on to him, and a babbling (12.) p☐oc☐ssi☐n of the

best stories in the world, sent from the (13.) h☐☐☐t of the earth to be told

at last to the (14.) ☐nsa☐i☐bl☐ sea.

As he sat on the grass and looked across the river, a dark hole in the bank

(15.) op☐☐sit☐, just above the water's edge, caught his eye, and dreamily he

fell to (16.) ☐ons☐d☐☐ing what a nice snug dwelling place it would make

for an animal with few wants and fond of a bijou riverside (17.) r☐sid☐☐ce,

above flood level and (18.) ☐emot☐ from noise and dust. As he gazed something

(19.) b☐i☐☐t and small seemed to twinkle down in the heart of it,

(20.) ☐an☐s☐ed, then twinkled once more like a tiny star.

33. FLOWERS AND HERBS

contribute	span	separately	delicate	exist
inspire	force	infloresence	over	blooms
vital	distinguished	considered	symbolise	people
admired	whereas	vegetables	amaze	growth

Write the correct word from the bank above to fill the space.

Animals and humans are not the only life (1.) _____ on our planet. Indeed, they would not be able to (2.) _____ at all if there were no plant life. Plants are not only (3.) _____ for our physical survival but also (4.) _____ to our happiness and emotional well-being.

Flowers - also called (5.) _____ or blossoms - are the most colourful part of a plant; many thousands of different varieties (6.) _____ and delight people all (7.) _____ the world. They can grow (8.) _____ on a plant or altogether in an (9.) _____. Many are fragrant as well as rich, vibrant and (10.) _____ in hue. Flowers are (11.) _____ and used by people to celebrate special occasions such as births, deaths and marriages. Some flowers are used to signal meanings; lilies can (12.) _____ life and roses make people think of love.

Many (13.) _____ enjoy growing flowers and gardening is (14.) _____ to be not only relaxing and good for spiritual (15.) _____, but also good physical exercise.

Did you know that people also eat some types of flowers? If you had broccoli, cauliflower or artichoke for your lunch today you were eating flower (16.) _____.

33. FLOWERS AND HERBS (CONT.)

Herbs are plants used for food flavouring, medicine or perfume. Herbs are (17.) _____ from spices in cooking. They are the leafy green part of a plant (18.) _____ a spice is a product from another part of the plant.

Flowers and herbs can (19.) _____ in us many philosophical ideas. For example, they have a very limited life (20.) _____ but spend their short lives making others happy.

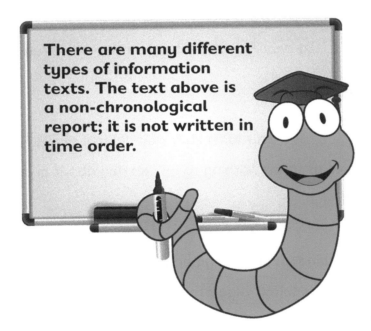

There are many different types of information texts. The text above is a non-chronological report; it is not written in time order.

34. THE DAY OF THE EXAM

Fill in the missing letters to complete the words in the following passage.

"Beep. . .Beep. . .Beep"

I whacked my alarm clock for the second time. It had (1.) ☐☐r☐v☐d, the day of my 11+ exam. After going to bed earlier than usual, I felt (2.) **re**☐☐**es**☐**ed** and ready for the challenge.

The night before, I had (3.) **s**☐**ste**☐☐**tic**☐☐**ly** put out everything for the day. These items (4.) ☐☐**cl**☐☐**ed** a water bottle (to keep me hydrated), three well (5.) **s**☐☐**rp**☐☐☐**d** pencils with rubbers on the end, a few extra erasers and a see-through pencil-case.

I had been (6.) ☐**rep**☐☐☐**ng** for a year and did feel slightly (7.) **a**☐**x**☐☐**us**. However, our teachers told us this is nothing to be worried about and some nerves are a (8.) ☐**os**☐☐☐**ve** sign.

After triple checking everything, my mum and dad (who seemed (9.) **c**☐**mp**☐**et**☐☐**y** calm!) suggested we leave soon. "Best to be early, in case parking is (10.) **pr**☐☐**lem**☐☐☐☐," stated Dad.

As we drove towards the school where I was taking my 11+ exam, I could see friends who I had (11.) **p**☐☐**cti**☐☐**d** with. That made me feel good as I knew they would be close by.

After arriving and taking a (12.) **l**☐☐**su**☐☐**ly** stroll towards the exam hall, my mum and dad kept giving me words of (13.) **re**☐☐☐**ura**☐☐**e**. "Just do your best dear," remarked Mum.

34. THE DAY OF THE EXAM (CONT.)

The exam seemed to go quickly and I (14.) ☐☐**te**☐☐**ted** every question. My best

friend and I chatted (15.) **br**☐☐☐**ly** about it. She said it was fine and I agreed.

My parents gave me a huge hug afterwards and (16.) ☐**ro**☐☐**sed** to take me

to watch a film at the cinema.

I felt (17.) **c**☐☐**t**☐☐**ted** with how the exam went and knew that all the

(18.) **pr**☐☐☐**ra**☐☐ **on** helped me (19.) **m**☐☐**si**☐☐**ly**.

I (20.) **per**☐☐☐**me**☐ to the best of my ability and now all I had to do was wait

and see.

35. GULLIVER'S TRAVELS
By Jonathan Swift

In this extract, Lemuel Gulliver recounts what happens after he is shipwrecked on the shores of Lilliput, a land inhabited by tiny humans.

leaping	roared	grow	same
sky	were	an	grass
all	inches	felt	hours
was	offended	downwards	depth
moving	a	houses	back

Write the correct word from the bank above to fill the space.

I swam as fortune directed me, and was pushed forward by wind and tide. I often let my legs drop, and could feel no bottom; but when I was almost gone, and able to struggle no longer, I found myself within my (1.) _____; by this time, the storm was much abated. I walked near a mile before I got to the shore, which was about eight o'clock in the evening. I then advanced forward near half a mile, but could not discover any sign of (2.) _____ or inhabitants; at least, I was in so weak a condition, that I did not observe them. I was extremely tired, and with that, and the heat of the weather, and about half a pint of brandy that I drank as I left the ship, I found myself much inclined to sleep.

I lay down on the (3.) _____, which was very short and soft, where I slept sounder than ever I remember to have done in my life. I reckoned about nine (4.) _____ passed; for when I awakened, it was just daylight. I attempted to rise, but was not able to stir; for, as I happened to lie on my (5.) _____, I found my arms and legs were strongly fastened on each side to the ground; and my hair, which was long and thick, tied down in the (6.) _____ manner. I likewise (7.) _____ several slender ligatures across my body, from my arm-pits to my thighs. I could only look upwards; the sun began to (8.) _____ hot, and the light (9.) _____ my eyes. I heard a confused noise about me; but in the posture I lay, could see nothing except the (10.) _____. In a little time, I felt something alive (11.) _____ on my left leg, which advancing

35. GULLIVER'S TRAVELS (CONT.)

gently forward over my breast, came almost up to my chin; when, bending my eyes

(12.) _____ as much as I could, I perceived it to be a human creature not six

(13.) _____ high, with a bow and (14.) _____ arrow in his hands and

(15.) _____ quiver at his back. In the meantime I felt at least forty more of the same

kind (as I conjectured) following the first. I (16.) _____ in the utmost astonishment,

and (17.) _____ so loud that they (18.) _____ ran back in a fright, and

some of them, as I was afterwards told, (19.) _____ hurt by the falls they got by

(20.) _____ from my sides upon the ground.

Don't forget to capitalise the initial letter if the word is at the start of a sentence.

PERFECT PLURALS 1

Help Billy complete these plurals. In Test 25, you will see 'wolves' is the plural of 'wolf'. While many words form their plural by adding '-es' or '-s', others have different rules.

1. monkey ....

2. ox ....

3. witch ....

4. tooth ....

5. goose ....

6. person ....

7. church ....

8. city ....

9. baby ....

10. shoal ....

If the word ends with a vowel + 'y' add only an 's', but if it ends in a consonant + 'y' remove the 'y' and add 'ies'. However note that this might not work for all words.

Teachitright Teaser: Can you find the plurals of any of the words above in the tests?

36. THE EMPEROR'S NEW CLOTHES 05:00
05 minutes
by Hans Christian Andersen

Mark the box with a pencil line next to the correct word to complete the sentence.

In this extract, the Emperor is fooled by some trickster merchants who persuade him that anyone who cannot see their cloth is stupid. He is eager to identify those people in his empire who are stupid, little suspecting that he could be one of them!

One day two swindlers came to this city; they made people believe that they were

weavers, and (1.) a. declared
b. decreased   that they could manufacture the
c. demanded

(2.) a. fabulous
b. finest   cloth to be imagined. Their colours and patterns, they said,
c. famous

(3.) a. where
b. were   not only exceptionally beautiful, but the clothes made of their
c. wear

material (4.) a. possessed
b. owed   the wonderful quality of being invisible to any man who
c. has

was (5.) a. unable
b. unfit   for his office or unpardonably stupid.
c. undeserved

"That must be wonderful cloth," thought the Emperor. "If I were to be

(6.) a. dressed
b. wearing   in a suit made of this cloth I (7.) a. shall
b. meant   be able to find
c. made   c. should

out (8.) a. witch
b. which   men in my empire were unfit for their places, and I could
c. what

(continued over)

36. THE EMPEROR'S NEW CLOTHES (CONT.)

(9.) ☐ a. extinguish
☐ b. distinguish   the clever from the stupid. I must have this cloth woven for
☐ c. relinquish

(10.) ☐ a. me
☐ b. them   without delay." And he gave a large (11.) ☐ a. cash
☐ c. you   ☐ b. sum   of
                                                                          ☐ c. lot

money to the swindlers, in advance, that they should set to work without any

loss of time. They set up two looms, and (12.) ☐ a. acted
☐ b. pretended   to be very hard
☐ c. tricked

at work, but they did nothing (13.) ☐ a. whoever
☐ b. wherever   on the looms. They asked
☐ c. whatever

for the finest silks and the most (14.) ☐ a. precious
☐ b. pressed   gold thread; all they got
☐ c. pretend

they (15.) ☐ a. done
☐ b. did   away with, and worked at the empty looms till late at night.
☐ c. do

"I should very much like to know how they are getting (16.) ☐ a. on
☐ b. done   with
☐ c. finished

the cloth," thought the Emperor. But he felt rather (17.) ☐ a. uneasy
☐ b. unable
☐ c. understandable

when he remembered that he who was not fit for his office could not see it.

Personally, he was of the (18.) ☐ a. option
☐ b. opinion   that he had nothing to fear, yet
☐ c. opposition

36. THE EMPEROR'S NEW CLOTHES (CONT.)

he thought it advisable to send somebody else first to see how matters

(19)　　a. stood
　　　　b. stand　　.
　　　　c. standing

"I shall send my honest old minister to the weavers," thought the Emperor. "He

　　　　a. how
can judge best (20.)　　b. who　　the stuff looks, for he is intelligent, and nobody
　　　　c. where

understands his office better than he."

The good old minister went into the room where the swindlers sat before the empty looms. "Heaven preserve us!" he thought, and opened his eyes wide, "I cannot see anything at all," but he did not say so.

You can use a process of elimination to narrow down your choices if you are confident that one of the three options are wrong.

37. JUST WILLIAM
By Richmal Crompton

07:00
07 minutes

Fill in the missing letters to complete the words in the following passage.

William is a mischievous – some might say naughty – boy. He is about to have some fun with a balloon.

William was feeling embittered with life in general. He was passing

(1.) **th**☐**o**☐**g**☐ one of his not infrequent periods of unpopularity. The climax

had come with the (2.) **g**☐☐**t** of sixpence bestowed on him by a

(3.) **t**☐**m**☐**d** aunt, who hoped thus to purchase his goodwill. With the

sixpence he had (4.) **b**☐☐☐**ht** a balloon adorned with the legs and head

of a duck fashioned in cardboard. This (5.) **co**☐☐**d** be blown up to its

fullest extent and then left to (6.) **su**☐**s**☐**d**☐. It took several minutes to

subside, and (7.) **d**☐☐☐**ng** those minutes it emitted a long-drawn-out and

high-pitched groan. The advantage of this was (8.) ☐**bvi**☐**u**☐. William

could blow it up to its fullest extent in private and leave it to subside in public

concealed (9.) **b**☐**n**☐**a**☐**h** his coat. While this was going on William

looked (10.) **r**☐☐**n**☐ as though in bewildered astonishment. He inflated it

(11.) **b**☐☐**o**☐**e** he went to breakfast. He then held it (12.) **f**☐☐**m**☐**y**

and secretly so as to keep it inflated till he was sitting at the table. Then

he let it subside. His mother (13.) ☐☐**ock**☐**d** over a cup of coffee, and

his father cut (14.) **h**☐☐**s**☐☐**f** with the bread knife. Ethel, his elder

sister, indulged in a mild form of nervous breakdown. William sat with a

(15.) ☐**ac**☐ of startled innocence. But nothing enraged his (16.) **f**☐**m**☐☐**y**

so much as William's expression of innocence. They fell (17.) ☐**p**☐**n** him, and

he defended himself as well as he could. Yes, he was (18.) **h**☐☐**d**☐☐**g**

the balloon under the table. Well, he'd (19.) **b**☐**o**☐**n** it up some time ago.

37. JUST WILLIAM (CONT.)

He couldn't keep it blown up for ever. He had to let the air out some time.

He couldn't help it making a noise when the air went out. It was the

(20.) ☐ a ☐ it was made. He hadn't made it. He set off to school with an air of

injured innocence — and the balloon.

If there are words in a passage that you have not come across before, it is worth looking them up and writing their meaning down. You can never know too many words!

38. THE RAILWAY CHILDREN
By Edith Nesbit

`05:00`
05 minutes

Mark the box with a pencil line next to the correct word to complete the sentence.

In this extract, the children are hunting, in sight of the railway lines, for wild cherries.

So they went (1.) □ a. astride
□ b. along   the fence towards the little swing gate
□ c. amongst

□ a. that
(2.) □ b. who   is at the top of these steps. And they were almost at the gate when
□ c. what

Bobbie said: —

"Hush. Stop! What's that?"

"That" was a very (3.) □ a. old
□ b. loud noise indeed — a soft noise, but (4.) □ a. quite
□ b. quiet
□ c. odd   □ c. queer

plainly to be heard (5.) □ a. threw
□ b. though   the sound of the wind in tree branches, and the
□ c. through

hum and whir of the telegraph (6.) □ a. poll.
□ b. wears. It (7.) □ a. is
□ c. wires.   □ b. were a sort of rustling,
□ c. was

whispering sound. As they listened it stopped, and then it (8.) □ a. begun
□ b. began again.
□ c. begins

And this time it did not stop, but it (9.) □ a. grows
□ b. grew   louder and more rustling and
□ c. growls

rumbling.

"Look," — cried Peter, suddenly — "the tree over (10.) □ a. there
□ b. their   !"
□ c. they're

38. THE RAILWAY CHILDREN (CONT.)

The tree he pointed at was (11.)
- a. wan
- b. won
- c. one

of those that have rough grey

(12.)
- a. leave
- b. leaf
- c. leaves

and white flowers. The (13.)
- a. berries
- b. buries
- c. berry

when they

come, are (14.)
- a. painted
- b. bright
- c. colour

scarlet, but if you pick (15.)
- a. them
- b. those
- c. then

they

(16.)
- a. discard
- b. discuss
- c. disappoint

you by turning black before you get them home. And, as Peter

pointed, the tree was moving — not just the way trees (17.)
- a. aught
- b. should
- c. ought

to move

when the wind blows through them, but all in one (18.)
- a. peace
- b. pierce
- c. piece

, as though it were

a (19.)
- a. lightly
- b. live
- c. loving

creature and were walking down the side of the cutting.

"It's moving!" cried Bobbie. "Oh, look! And so are the others. It's like the

(20.)
- a. words
- b. woods
- c. would

in *Macbeth*."

Look carefully at the tense of the words. Some very slight changes in spelling make all the difference, e.g. I begin, I began, I have begun; I grow, I grew, I have grown.

39. THE BOOK OF DRAGONS

05:00
05 minutes

By Edith Nesbit

pleased	lizard	another	shiny	long
care	family	fished	lunch	fast
drop	brushes	usual	flopped	forward
each	afternoon	finer	earwig	stretching

Write the correct word from the bank above to fill the space.

When Effie's father removes something from her eye, he looks at it with great curiosity. Under his microscope it is revealed to be an unusual winged creature.

"You might give me sixpence, Daddy," said Effie, "because I did bring you the new specimen. I took great care of it inside my eye, and my eye *does* hurt."

The doctor was so (1.) _____ with the new specimen that he gave

Effie a shilling, and presently the professor stepped round. He stayed to

(2.) _____, and he and the doctor quarrelled very happily all the

(3.) _____ about the name and the (4.) _____ of the

thing that had come out of Effie's eye.

But at teatime (5.) _____ thing happened. Effie's brother Harry

(6.) _____ something out of his tea, which he thought at first was an

(7.) _____. He was just getting ready to (8.) _____ it

on the floor, and end its life in the (9.) _____ way, when it shook itself in

the spoon — spread two wet wings, and (10.) _____ onto the tablecloth.

There it sat, stroking itself with its feet and (11.) _____ its wings, and

Harry said: "Why, it's a tiny newt!"

The professor leaned (12.) _____ before the doctor could say a

word. "I'll give you half a crown for it Harry, my lad," he said, speaking very

39. THE BOOK OF DRAGONS (CONT.)

(13.) _____; and then he picked it up with (14.) _____

on his handkerchief.

"It is a new specimen," he said, "and (15.) _____ than yours, Doctor."

It was a tiny lizard, about half an inch long — with scales and wings.

So now the doctor and the professor (16.) _____ had a specimen, and

they were both very pleased. But before (17.) _____ these specimens

began to seem less valuable. For the next morning, when the knife-boy was cleaning the

doctor's boots, he suddenly dropped the (18.) _____ and the boot and the

blacking, and screamed out that he was burnt. And from inside the boot came crawling a

(19.) _____ as big as a kitten, with large, (20.) _____

wings.

"Why," said Effie, "I know what it is. It is a dragon like the one St. George killed."

Passages which contain lots of direct speech can be more confusing because of all the extra punctuation as well as the different word choices. Just read through carefully and you will begin to see how the writing flows.

40. TOM BROWN'S SCHOOL DAYS

By Thomas Hughes

Mark the box with a pencil line next to the correct word to complete the sentence. ▭

Tom Brown has just become a pupil at Rugby School. In this extract, he is now about to watch his first football match, which they play very differently there!

"But why do you wear white trousers in November?" said Tom. He had been struck by this peculiarity in the costume of almost all the School-house boys.

"Why, bless us, don't you know? No; I forgot. Why, to-day's the School-house match.

▭ a. hole

Our house plays the (1.) ▭ b. whole   of the School at football. And we all

▭ c. total

▭ a. wear

(2.) ▭ b. where   white trousers, to show 'em', we don't care for hacks. You're in luck

▭ c. ware

to come to-day. You just will see a match; and Brooke's going to let me play in quarters.

▭ a. more

That's (3.) ▭ b. moor   than he'll do for any other lower-school boy, except James, and

▭ c. less

he's fourteen."

"Who's Brooke?"

▭ a. calling

"Why, that big fellow who (4.) ▭ b. called   over at dinner, to be sure. He's cock of the

▭ c. kept

school, and head of the School-house side, and the best kick and charger in Rugby."

▭ a. tennis

"Oh, but do show me where they play. And tell me about it. I love (5.) ▭ b. football so,

▭ c. running

and have played all my life. Won't Brooke let me play?"

▭ a. know

"Not he," said East, with some indignation. "Why, you don't (6.) ▭ b. no   the rules;

▭ c. now

40. TOM BROWN'S SCHOOL DAYS (CONT.)

you'll be a month (7.) [ ] a. teaching
[ ] b. learning   them. And then it's no joke playing-up in a
[ ] c. practising

match, I can tell you — quite another thing from your private school (8.)
[ ] a. jokes
[ ] b. gamer .
[ ] c. games

Why, there's been (9.) [ ] a. too
[ ] b. to   collar-bones broken this half, and a dozen fellows
[ ] c. two

lamed. And last year a fellow had his leg broken."

Tom (10.) [ ] a. listening
[ ] b. listened   with the profoundest respect to this chapter of
[ ] c. heard

(11.) [ ] a. accidents
[ ] b. excitements , and followed East across the level ground till they came to a
[ ] c. matches

sort of gigantic gallows of two poles, eighteen feet high, fixed upright in the

(12.) [ ] a. wall
[ ] b. ground some fourteen feet apart, with a cross-bar running from one to the
[ ] c. goal

other at the height of ten feet or thereabouts.

"This is one of the (13.) [ ] a. nets,"
[ ] b. goalies," said East, "and you see the other, across there,
[ ] c. goals,"

right opposite, under the Doctor's wall. Well, the match is for the best of three goals;

whichever side kicks two goals (14.) [ ] a. loses
[ ] b. draws : and it won't do, you
[ ] c. wins

(continued over)

40. TOM BROWN'S SCHOOL DAYS (CONT.)

☐ a. sea

(15.) ☐ b. see , just to kick the ball through these posts — it must go over the

☐ c. look

☐ a. over

cross-bar; any height'll do, so long as it's (16.) ☐ b. under the posts. You'll have to

☐ c. between

stay in goal to touch the ball when it rolls behind the posts, because if the other side

☐ a. play

touch it they have a try at goal. Then we fellows in quarters, we (17.) ☐ b. jump just

☐ c. sit

☐ a. here

about in front of goal (18.) ☐ b. hear , and have to turn the ball and kick it back before

☐ c. listen

the big fellows on the other side can follow it up. And in front of us all the big fellows

play, and that's where the scrummages are mostly."

☐ a. struggled

Tom's respect increased as he (19.) ☐ b. struggling to make out his friend's

☐ c. struggle

technicalities, and the other set to work to

☐ a. explain

(20.) ☐ b. explained the mysteries of "off

☐ c. explaining

your side," "drop-kicks," "punts," "places," and

the other intricacies of the great science of
football.

If you have read and understood this passage you can really see how much fun the boys had at school, but what a dangerous sport rugby football was!

PERFECT PLURALS 2

Here is another 'Perfect plurals' page to help you to practise and test your knowledge of plurals.

Remember that 'plural' means more than one. Most words add an 's' at the end to show there's more than one, for example *glove* becomes *gloves*. However, some words follow different rules, for example *berry* becomes *berries*. There are plenty of rules to learn for plurals. For example:

- For words ending in 'y', if there is a consonant before 'y', change the 'y' to 'i' before adding 'es' (e.g. body becomes bodies).

- If there is a vowel before the 'y', just add 's' (e.g. *boy* becomes *boys*).

- Some words which end in 'fe' or 'f' change to 'v' before adding 'ies' (e.g. *knife* becomes *knives*).

- Words ending in 'x', 'sh', 'ch', 's' or 'ss' just add 'es' (e.g. *brush* becomes *brushes*).

It's important to realise that there are words that don't fit this rule: for example, *chief – chiefs*. To help with these exceptions to the rule, listen for the change in sound.

See if you can complete the table below using the rules above.

Word	Plural	Word	Plural
wolf		leaf	
sack		finger	
queue		stadium	
box		fly	
sheep		search	
curtain		recess	

Check at the back of the book to see if you followed the plural rules correctly.

SECTION 5:
GLOSSARY AND ANSWERS

GLOSSARY

Abbreviation – the shortened form of a word or phrase.

Abstract noun – an abstract noun is a type of noun that refers to something with which a person cannot physically interact.

Adjective – a word that adds information about a noun or pronoun.

Adverb – a word that modifies a sentence, verb, adverb or adjective.

Antonym – a word that means the opposite of another.

Characterisation – the process by which an author reveals the personality of a human being or creature.

Classic – something judged over a period of time to be of the highest quality and an outstanding example of its kind.

Collective noun – a noun that is singular in form but that refers to a group of people or things, e.g. 'crowd' or 'army'.

Concrete noun – a concrete noun is the name of something or someone that we experience through our senses; sight, hearing, smell, touch or taste. Most nouns are concrete nouns. The opposite of a concrete noun is an abstract noun.

Conjunction – a word or group of words that connects words, phrases, or clauses; for example 'and', 'if' and 'but'.

Consonant – any letter of the alphabet that is not a vowel.

Contemporary – existing or occurring at the present time.

Context – the words before and after a word or passage in a piece of writing that contribute to its meaning.

Digraph – a combination of two letters representing one sound.

Elimination – the removal of something that is unwanted.

Grammar – the study of the way words are used to make sentences.

Homonym – a word pronounced and spelt the same as another but having a different meaning.

Homophone – a word which sounds the same as another word but with a different meaning and spelling.

Idiom – an idiom is a word or phrase that is not taken literally.

Inference – the act or process of reaching a conclusion by reasoning from evidence.

Mnemonic – a way of helping to remember certain facts or large amounts of information.

Non-chronological report – a non-chronological report is a piece of text that isn't written in time order.

Noun – a word that refers to a person, place or thing.

GLOSSARY

Partial – something that is incomplete.

Plural – consisting of more than one.

Possessive – showing a relationship where one thing belongs to another.

Preposition – a word used before a noun or pronoun to relate it to the other words.

Pronoun – a word that can replace a noun in a sentence.

Prose – ordinary spoken or written language in contrast to poetry.

Punctuation – the marks used in writing to separate words in sentences in order to clarify meaning.

Singular – denoting only one of something.

Synonym – a word that means the same, or almost the same, as another word.

Tense – the form taken by a verb to show whether something happened in the past, present or future.

Verb – a word that is used to indicate the occurrence or performance of an action.

Vowel – one of five letters: A, E, I, O and U.

Answers Section 1: Multiple choice options

Test 1: The Restless Earth

1	b	our
2	a	phrase
3	b	walk
4	a	learn
5	b	these
6	a	Earth's
7	a	Scientists
8	c	have
9	c	lies
10	b	between
11	b	builds
12	c	slip
13	c	in
14	c	bring
15	c	its
16	b	are
17	a	Here
18	b	and
19	b	onto
20	a	buried

Test 2: Treasure Island

1	b	aside
2	a	promised
3	a	seafaring
4	b	applied
5	a	wage
6	a	through
7	b	was
8	b	repeat
9	a	personage
10	b	scarcely
11	a	stormy
12	a	cove
13	b	would
14	b	expressions
15	a	now

16	b	had
17	c	nightmares
18	b	dear
19	b	monthly
20	c	fancies

Test 3: Pinocchio

1	b	stubborn
2	b	twinkling
3	a	desperation
4	a	pry
5	b	deep
6	a	spat
7	c	himself
8	b	leaping
9	a	swiftly
10	b	pursuers
11	a	exhausted
12	b	enormous
13	c	could
14	b	fell
15	b	giving
16	b	piled
17	a	began
18	a	higher
19	c	ground
20	a	warning

Test 4: Trains

1	c	built
2	a	inventions
3	a	were
4	b	incredible
5	c	technology
6	b	developed
7	a	quantities
8	b	reachable
9	a	condensed
10	c	definitely

11	a	efficient
12	a	produce
13	c	cargo
14	b	appeared
15	a	kilometres
16	c	tunnels
17	a	underground
18	b	network
19	b	wavered
20	c	connects

Test 5: The Butterfly Lion

1	a	deciding
2	b	heard
3	b	again
4	b	stood
5	a	scrutinised
6	c	piercing
7	a	rain
8	b	gentler
9	a	leash
10	a	ominous
11	c	hackles
12	b	you're
13	a	property
14	a	accusingly
15	b	aside
16	a	anything
17	a	to
18	a	can't
19	b	stand
20	a	We'll

Test 6: The Adventures of Maya the Bee

1	a	when
2	b	appear
3	b	over
4	a	shriek
5	a	his
6	c	done
7	a	never
8	b	fate
9	a	comfort
10	a	Each
11	a	back
12	b	honestly
13	a	it
14	b	stares
15	b	blade
16	c	can't
17	c	was
18	a	bound
19	c	bend
20	b	Frightened

Test 7: Indira's Pets

1	b	all
2	a	prided
3	a	attention
4	b	tire
5	c	however
6	c	around
7	c	his
8	b	vexed
9	c	clean
10	a	hers
11	a	but
12	b	fare
13	a	fateful
14	c	reached

15	a	notify
16	c	tail
17	c	another
18	a	that
19	b	soap
20	c	ministrations

Test 8: The Story of Dr Dolittle

1	b	whole
2	a	sea
3	b	ship
4	c	carried
5	a	shooting
6	b	sailed
7	b	warmer
8	c	see
9	b	shade
10	c	their
11	b	swimming
12	c	too
13	b	under
14	b	boat
15	b	saw
16	b	coming
17	a	told
18	a	were
19	b	monkeys
20	c	would

Test 9: The Fir Tree

1	c	stood
2	a	one
3	a	him
4	c	around
5	c	wanted
6	c	didn't
7	b	fresh
8	b	about

9	c	whole
10	b	them
11	a	young
12	b	bear
13	a	shot
14	c	another
15	b	Were
16	c	able
17	a	breeze
18	b	sailed
19	a	angry
20	c	delightful

Test 10: The Phoenix and the Carpet

1	b	something
2	b	there
3	a	cracking
4	c	two
5	a	four
6	c	mouth
7	a	rose
8	b	warm
9	a	looked
10	a	may
11	c	going
12	a	feathers
13	c	hurried
14	b	came
15	a	others
16	b	for
17	c	saying
18	a	least
19	c	know
20	b	which

Answers Section 2: Partial Words

Test 11: The Planets

1	wonder
2	sometimes
3	guess
4	sustain
5	neither
6	creatures
7	receives
8	from
9	largest
10	enormous
11	around
12	luminous
13	circling
14	called
15	favourite
16	stunning
17	surrounded
18	awesome
19	sadly
20	fascination

Test 12: David Copperfield

1	informed
2	evening
3	fetched
4	comfortable
5	presence
6	stout
7	chair
8	teeth
9	fiery
10	veins
11	bald
12	circumstance
13	whisper
14	angry
15	thicker

16	beckoning
17	stepfather
18	character
19	pinching
20	ferocious

Test 13: Peter Pan

1	extremely
2	loveliest
3	answered
4	ordinary
5	recovered
6	appalled
7	pleasantly
8	courteously
9	frightfully
10	smiling
11	exactly
12	sewn
13	patronisingly
14	ignorant
15	exulting
16	daresay
17	creased
18	indifferent
19	appearances
20	rapturously

Test 14: My first day at school

1	beautiful
2	imagined
3	Believe
4	optimism
5	pounding
6	effect
7	accompanied
8	mingling
9	strange

10	return
11	disappeared
12	anxiously
13	potatoes
14	jiggled
15	perk
16	questions
17	unfortunately
18	relieved
19	inwardly
20	pleasure

Test 15: War Horse

1	height
2	approached
3	immediately
4	intrigued
5	against
6	touched
7	smoothed
8	while
9	smartest
10	world
11	salted
12	brought
13	believe
14	understand
15	broadly
16	stroked
17	rhymes
18	because
19	promise
20	Obstinate

Test 16: The Adventures of Tom Sawyer

1	always
2	another
3	holiday
4	thinking
5	occurred
6	school
7	system
8	began
9	considerable
10	something
11	teeth
12	lucky
13	argument
14	would
15	remembered
16	certain
17	finger
18	eagerly
19	However
20	groaning

Test 17: The Jungle Book

1	feeling
2	strong
3	branches
4	staring
5	woke
6	cries
7	bounded
8	tooth
9	triumph
10	upper
11	follow
12	admire
13	cunning
14	nobody

15	describe
16	laid
17	necessary
18	swung
19	weight
20	glimpses

Test 18: The Frog Prince

1	wanted
2	youngest
3	beautiful
4	shone
5	castle
6	under
7	when
8	daughter
9	seemed
10	throw
11	favourite
12	happened
13	instead
14	which
15	ground
16	edge
17	eyes
18	could
19	comforted
20	voice

Test 19: Rebecca of Sunnybrook Farm

1	door
2	unlocked
3	piece
4	stairs
5	would
6	wear
7	after
8	pink

9	two
10	tied
11	slipped
12	fasten
13	girls
14	school
15	wrap
16	coming
17	downstairs
18	cheeks
19	hair
20	minutes

Test 20: The Velveteen Rabbit

1	cupboard
2	thought
3	about
4	ideas
5	lived
6	anything
7	existed
8	understood
9	wooden
10	pretended
11	poor
12	insignificant
13	patches
14	underneath
15	tail
16	bead
17	their
18	would
19	magic
20	wonderful

Answers Section 3: Word Banks

Test 21: The Railway Children

1	suppose
2	ordinary
3	their
4	coloured
5	tiled
6	convenience
7	eldest
8	favourites
9	engineer
10	youngest
11	extremely
12	there
13	Besides
14	aloud
15	occasions
16	refurnishing
17	merry
18	unjust
19	excellent
20	interestingly

Test 22: The Wonderful City of Oz

1	protected
2	dazzled
3	lined
4	studded
5	glittering
6	panes
7	tint
8	dressed
9	greenish
10	spoke
11	offered
12	clothes
13	lemonade
14	carried

15	pushed
16	contented
17	prosperous
18	building
19	uniform
20	answered

Test 23: Deep Sea Wildlife

1	largest
2	sunlight
3	blackness
4	extraordinary
5	adapted
6	survive
7	surface
8	enormous
9	teeth
10	grabbing
11	stomachs
12	themselves
13	sieve
14	searching
15	particles
16	Hundreds
17	patrol
18	similar
19	relatives
20	fishing

Test 24: Australia

1	Located
2	hemisphere
3	varied
4	vast
5	interior
6	expanse
7	formerly
8	impressive
9	renowned

10	shallow
11	world's
12	marine
13	magnificent
14	shoals
15	dart
16	vivid
17	colony
18	inhabitants
19	city's
20	spans

Test 25: White Fang

1	attention
2	lunging
3	observing
4	strained
5	intruder
6	decoy
7	spluttering
8	of
9	darkness
10	announced
11	animal's
12	ought
13	had
14	cogitated
15	baby
16	wolves
17	wolf's
18	many's
19	cartridges
20	sure

Answers Section 3: Word Banks

Test 26: The Selfish Giant

1	afternoon
2	used
3	soft
4	there
5	beautiful
6	broke
7	bore
8	sweetly
9	stop
10	order
11	here
12	cried
13	friend
14	ogre
15	over
16	conversation
17	determined
18	gruff
19	nobody
20	wall

Test 27: Heidi

1	steps
2	joyously
3	firm
4	wherever
5	life
6	well
7	fulfilled
8	reached
9	wealth
10	dry
11	perfume
12	exquisite
13	grasp
14	brim
15	sleep

16	flew
17	goats
18	glad
19	mightily
20	again

Test 28: Robin Hood

1	walking
2	spanned
3	one
4	midst
5	anger
6	arrow
7	arms
8	unbuckled
9	falls
10	into
11	waded
12	blew
13	horn
14	river
15	stranger
16	tumbled
17	would
18	their
19	hand
20	name

Test 29: The Secret Garden

1	hopped
2	waistcoat
3	breast
4	pretty
5	human
6	forgot
7	something
8	flowers
9	together

10	earth
11	worm
12	hole
13	knowing
14	buried
15	brass
16	flew
17	hand
18	key
19	frightened
20	whisper

Test 30: The Elephant's Child

1	helped
2	throwing
3	could
4	wood
5	winked
6	seen
7	person
8	tail
9	politely
10	spanked
11	hairy
12	including
13	more
14	tears
15	bank
16	crocodile
17	whisper
18	close
19	little
20	useful

Answers Section 4: Mixed Cloze Passages

Test 31: A Christmas Carol

1	a	distinguish
2	c	opaque
3	a	pierce
4	b	listened
5	c	astonishment
6	a	past
7	b	preposterous
8	c	beat
9	c	slept
10	a	scrambled
11	b	obliged
12	c	foggy
13	a	unquestionably
14	a	possession
15	b	relief
16	b	security
17	a	perplexed
18	c	endeavoured
19	b	exceedingly
20	a	inquiry

Test 32: The Wind in the Willows

1	complete
2	aimlessly
3	sinuous
4	laugh
5	shook
6	shiver
7	bewitched
8	trotted
9	holds
10	exhausted
11	chattered
12	procession
13	heart
14	insatiable

15	opposite
16	considering
17	residence
18	remote
19	bright
20	vanished

Test 33: Flowers and herbs

1	force
2	exist
3	vital
4	contribute
5	blooms
6	amaze
7	over
8	separately
9	inflorescence
10	delicate
11	admired
12	symbolise
13	people
14	considered
15	growth
16	vegetables
17	distinguished
18	whereas
19	inspire
20	span

Test 34: The day of the exam

1	arrived
2	refreshed
3	systematically
4	included
5	sharpened
6	preparing
7	anxious

8	positive
9	completely
10	problematic
11	practised
12	leisurely
13	reassurance
14	attempted
15	briefly
16	promised
17	contented
18	preparation
19	massively
20	performed

Test 35: Gulliver's Travels

1	depth
2	houses
3	grass
4	hours
5	back
6	same
7	felt
8	grow
9	offended
10	sky
11	moving
12	downwards
13	inches
14	an
15	a
16	was
17	roared
18	all
19	were
20	leaping

Test 36: The Emperor's New Clothes

1	a	declared
2	b	finest
3	b	were
4	a	possessed
5	b	unfit
6	a	dressed
7	c	should
8	b	which
9	b	distinguish
10	a	me
11	b	sum
12	b	pretended
13	c	whatever
14	a	precious
15	b	did
16	a	on
17	a	uneasy
18	b	opinion
19	a	stood
20	a	how

Test 37: Just William

1	through
2	gift
3	timid
4	bought
5	could
6	subside
7	during
8	obvious
9	beneath
10	round
11	before
12	firmly
13	knocked
14	himself

15	face
16	family
17	upon
18	holding
19	blown
20	way

Test 38: The Railway Children

1	b	along
2	a	that
3	c	odd
4	a	quite
5	c	through
6	c	wires
7	c	was
8	b	began
9	b	grew
10	a	there
11	c	one
12	c	leaves
13	a	berries
14	b	bright
15	a	them
16	c	disappoint
17	c	ought
18	c	piece
19	b	live
20	b	woods

Test 39: The Book of Dragons

1	pleased
2	lunch
3	afternoon
4	family
5	another
6	fished
7	earwig

8	drop
9	usual
10	flopped
11	stretching
12	forward
13	fast
14	care
15	finer
16	each
17	long
18	brushes
19	lizard
20	shiny

Test 40: Tom Brown's School Days

1	b	whole
2	b	wear
3	a	more
4	b	called
5	b	football
6	a	know
7	b	learning
8	c	games
9	c	two
10	b	listened
11	a	accidents
12	b	ground
13	c	goals
14	c	wins
15	b	see
16	c	between
17	a	play
18	a	here
19	a	struggled
20	a	explain

Answers: Billy's Fun Vocabulary Pages

Page 18: Helpful Homophones

1	our
2	inn
3	hear
4	threw
5	wood
6	deer
7	past
8	beet
9	berry
10	prophet

Page 35: Tricky Tenses

1	fly
2	bought
3	blown
4	bring
5	broke
6	bitten
7	build
8	caught
9	drunk
10	draw

Page 47: Super Synonyms

1	colossal
2	radiant
3	savage
4	rotund
5	fascinated
6	instantly
7	shocked
8	uneducated
9	advantage
10	combining

u	a	t	r	b	x	e	s	a	l	y	p
y	n	s	h	o	c	k	e	d	a	l	l
l	v	e	o	s	g	n	a	v	q	t	f
t	i	w	d	t	o	e	d	a	s	n	a
n	o	n	a	u	g	h	s	n	b	a	s
a	v	n	e	s	c	a	r	t	t	t	c
t	a	l	y	r	o	a	o	a	n	s	i
s	k	r	e	f	l	e	t	g	a	n	n
n	b	e	l	h	o	i	u	e	i	i	a
i	n	p	o	u	s	c	n	k	d	g	t
e	g	a	v	a	s	n	d	p	a	e	e
r	s	g	m	e	a	d	z	o	r	s	d
m	t	d	u	t	l	j	r	s	a	h	c
s	c	o	m	b	i	n	i	n	g	e	t

Answers: Billy's Fun Vocabulary Pages

Page 68: Awesome Antonyms

Down

1	dissatisfied
2	dull
5	border
9	miserable

Across

3	miniscule
4	ailing
6	deep
7	disloyal
8	unlike
10	modest
11	variable
12	exposed

Well done; now see how you did on the marking chart on the next page.

Page 80: Awesome Adjectives

1	hilarious
2	idle
3	mysterious
4	dreary
5	negative
6	angry
7	leafy
8	ancient
9	energetic
10	flimsy

Page 92: Perfect Plurals 1

1	monkeys
2	oxen
3	witches
4	teeth
5	geese
6	people
7	churches
8	cities
9	babies
10	shoals

Page 105: Perfect Plurals 2

Word	Plural	Word	Plural
wolf	wolves	leaf	leaves
sack	sacks	finger	fingers
queue	queues	stadium	stadiums or stadia
box	boxes	fly	flies
sheep	sheep	search	searches
curtain	curtains	recess	recesses

Marking Chart

Fill in the tables below with your results from each test. Each test is out of 20 with a total of 100 questions in each set of five tests.

Multiple Choice Options

	Test 1	Test 2	Test 3	Test 4	Test 5	Total
Score	/20	/20	/20	/20	/20	/100

	Test 6	Test 7	Test 8	Test 9	Test 10	Total
Score	/20	/20	/20	/20	/20	/100

Partial Words

	Test 11	Test 12	Test 13	Test 14	Test 15	Total
Score	/20	/20	/20	/20	/20	/100

	Test 16	Test 17	Test 18	Test 19	Test 20	Total
Score	/20	/20	/20	/20	/20	/100

Word Banks

	Test 21	Test 22	Test 23	Test 24	Test 25	Total
Score	/20	/20	/20	/20	/20	/100

	Test 26	Test 27	Test 28	Test 29	Test 30	Total
Score	/20	/20	/20	/20	/20	/100

Mixed Cloze Passages

	Test 31	Test 32	Test 33	Test 34	Test 35	Total
Score	/20	/20	/20	/20	/20	/100

	Test 36	Test 37	Test 38	Test 39	Test 40	Total
Score	/20	/20	/20	/20	/20	/100

Progress Grid

Colour the chart below with your total mark from each section to see how well you have done.

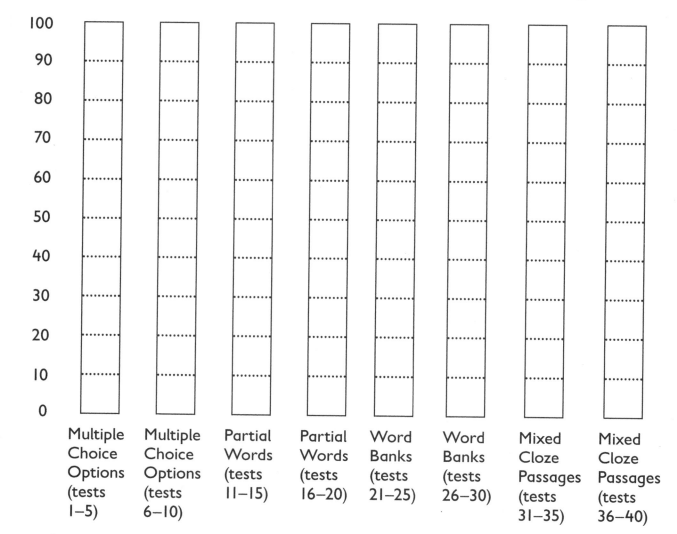

Read the statements below for some hints and tips.

Below 30%:   Remember to read the passage thoroughly to ensure it makes sense. Retry the passages and continue to build your vocabulary.

31% to 50%   Read ahead of the gaps to help with the contextual clues.

51% to 70%   Good effort. Continue to build your vocabulary by learning word definitions and synonyms.

71% to 90%   Well done. Keep enhancing your word knowledge.

91% +   You're a Cloze star. Keep up the hard work.